Angel Classics

T0086692

THE RATCATCHER

MARINA TSVETAEVA is now regarded as one of the greatest Russian poets OF the twentieth century, along with Blok, Pasternak, Mandelstam and Akhmatova. Born in Moscow in 1892, of a classicist father, who became famous as the founder of what is now the Pushkin Museum of Fine Arts, and a pianist mother who wanted her to have the musical career she herself had renounced, 'born not into life but into music', Tsvetaeva wrote poetry from childhood on and at the age of seventeen published a volume of poems at her own expense which got some positive reviews. At nineteen she married Sergey Efron, OF a family which had been associated with the revolutionary terrorist organisation The People's Will; she gave birth to two daughters, in 1912 and 1917. In the Civil War of 1918-20, Sergey joined the White Army; Marina, alone, impoverished and too impractical to hold down a job, placed her children in a home, where the younger one died of starvation.

In May 1922 she left Russia. After a few months in Berlin she moved to a suburb of Prague, rejoining her husband. Here she wrote most of *The Ratcatcher*, and her son Georgy was born. In November 1925 she moved definitively to Paris, where she wrote Canto 6 of *The Ratcatcher*. Living mostly in suburbs and in relative poverty, struggling with daily life and writing constantly, Tsvetaeva remained in France until her fatal return to Russia in 1939, at the height of the purges and persecutions, to join her husband who had become a Soviet sympathiser (he had actually begun to work for the secret police, although this was unknown to her). Her sister (who had not emigrated) had been arrested and sent to a camp; soon after their arrival her husband was arrested and executed; her daughter was arrested and also sent to the camps. She had few friends and little income; the atmosphere was sinister. In 1941, in the desolate Tatar town of Yelabuga to which she had been evacuated, Tsvetaeva hanged herself. Her body was buried in an unmarked common grave. Shortly afterwards, her son was conscripted into the army and shot.

Marina Tsvetaeva's large oeuvre – much of it written and first published in emigration – consists of some dozen books of short poems, as many long poems (*poemy*), eight plays, and numerous prose works.

ANGELA LIVINGSTONE is a Professor of Literature at the University of Essex. Among her publications are three books on Pasternak and a life and work of Lou Andreas-Salomé; also translations of a selection of essays by Tsvetaeva, *Art in the Light of Conscience* (1992) and (with Robert and Elizabeth Chandler) a volume of ten stories by Andrey Platonov, *The Return* (1999).

MARINA TSVETAEVA

The Ratcatcher

A lyrical satire

Translated
with an introduction and notes by
ANGELA LIVINGSTONE

NORTHWESTERN UNIVERSITY PRESS
Evanston, Illinois

Northwestern University Press
www.nupress.northwestern.edu

Translation, introduction, and notes
copyright © 1999 by Angela Livingstone.
Published 1999 by Angel Books. Northwestern University Press edition pubished
2000 by arrangement with Angel Books. All rights reserved.

ISBN-13: 978-0-8101-1816-4
ISBN-10: 0-8101-1816-5

Typeset in Great Britain by Ray Perry

For Alan

Contents

Acknowledgements

Above all I wish to thank Robert Chandler for reading, over several years, draft after draft of this translation, sending each one back with immensely helpful criticisms and ideas and suggesting many successful formulations.

I am grateful to Valentina Coe and to Nadezhda Bourova for helping me sort out innumerable Russian-language problems; to Irma Kudrova in St Petersburg and to Anna Saakyants in Moscow for sharing with me some of their profound knowledge of Tsvetaeva's work; to Susan Biver, Clive Hart, Kay Stevenson and Rod Wooden for their detailed responses to my text; to my son Ben and to my daughter Sonia for valuable discussions of this book; and to Rodney and Krystyna Livingstone for researching particular questions. Many others have helped with replies to my queries or comments on parts of the translation; my warm gratitude goes to them all.

Further I would like to thank Daniel Weissbort who published passages from *The Ratcatcher* in progress in *Modern Poetry in Translation*, no. 10, Winter 1996, and made me feel I could go on to translate the whole *poema*; and, especially, my present publisher Antony Wood for his many creative suggestions and his warm encouragement during the later stages of the work.

My thanks are due, also, to the Department of Literature, University of Essex, for a grant of money enabling me to visit the town of Hameln, and to the Director and the Librarian of the Hameln Museum for access to their collection of books and pamphlets about the Ratcatcher legend.

A.L.

Introduction

And now he is ready, having raised to his lips the reed, his
innocent fife, to tell you things you had better not listen to . . .

ALEXANDER BLOK, 'On Lyric Poetry', 1907

What shall I do with this measurelessness
In a world of measures?

MARINA TSVETAEVA, 'The Poet', 1923

MANY OF THE WRITERS now recognised as the greatest of the twentieth
century were unable to publish during the Soviet period and were more or
less severely persecuted. Marina Tsvetaeva (pronounced Tsvctacva) was
doubly *non grata* – for her White sympathies and for having emigrated.
Her work was not published substantially in Soviet Russia until 1965 and
even then it was censored and was hard to obtain. To generations of Rus-
sia poetry-readers she was unavailable. The poet Irina Ratushinskaya,
born a Soviet citizen in 1954, writes that it was not until she was twenty-
four that, suddenly able to borrow some rare books for just one week, she
'read almost simultaneously . . . Mandelstam, Tsvetaeva, Pasternak! They
literally knocked me off my feet, physically, giving me a fever and delir-
ium.'[1] *The Ratcatcher* was especially harshly cut, some 265 lines being
taken out of the 1965 edition to prevent Soviet readers associating the rats
with the Bolsheviks. It is only since the advent of *perestroika* in 1986 and
the freedom of research, criticism and publishing which it brought, that
this work has at last come into its own in Russia.

Although she admired the Symbolist Blok and the Futurist
Mayakovsky (whom she praised despite the general émigré hostility to
everything Soviet), loved and felt close to the modernist neo-Romantic
Pasternak, revered the more classical Mandelstam and Anna Akhmatova
(that other celebrated Russian woman poet with whom she is sometimes
fruitlessly compared), Tsvetaeva is not, finally, like any of them. She wrote
poems to, and prose about, all these poets, and she did have something in
common with most of them, sharing, for instance, the Symbolist convic-

tion of another 'higher' dimension of being, Pasternak's belief in a universal force of inspiration (she too can be called a 'Romantic'), and so much of Mayakovsky's poetic manner that she has been called a 'female Mayakovsky'. Nonetheless, her voice is unmistakably her own. While every important poet is *sui generis*, one wants to say so about Tsvetaeva with more emphasis than usual.

An emotional but not a 'feminine' poet, she avoids all mellifluous sentimentality and instead loves, hates, lauds, castigates, laments, marvels, aspires . . . with a kind of unflinching physicality, always pushing passions and stances to the point at which they will be fully revealed. Brodsky wrote (of both her verse and her prose) that 'her speech almost always begins . . . in the highest register, at its uppermost limit, after which only descent or, at best, a plateau is conceivable. However, the timbre of her voice was so tragic that it ensured a sensation of rising no matter how long the sound lasted.'[2]

Tsvetaeva's verse is rich in such features as conspicuous enjambement, abrupt self-interruption, exclamation and ellipsis, and has great rhetorical diversity. The powerful rhythms are usually the first thing to make an impact on the reader, and then the unexpected imagery and the tense, knotty complexity of much of the syntax. She makes nothing easy, but requires her reader to be her equal, whether as co-mountaineer, or sparring partner, or simply strenuous listener.

Responses to *The Ratcatcher*

Most critics and readers concur in placing *The Ratcatcher* (*Krysolov*) at the peak of Tsvetaeva's work. 'This dazzlingly brilliant poem', her 'magnum opus': this judgement in 1985 by Simon Karlinsky, who had introduced Tsvetaeva to Western readers nineteen years earlier, has been echoed by many others. In Russia the well-known critic Pavel Antokolsky, almost the first to write publicly of it there, said in 1966: 'The summit of her mature work was of course the poema *The Ratcatcher*.'[3] It is now greatly praised by Russian critics.

Yet in its time it was almost ignored. Only two contemporary responses are worth quoting. The literary critic and historian D.S. Mirsky (like Tsvetaeva, a post-1917 émigré and, like her, eventually returning to Russia to his ruin) reviewed it in 1926, the year it appeared, saying it was 'not merely . . . a verbal structure astounding in its richness and shapeliness, but also a serious "political" (in the widest sense) and ethical satire, perhaps destined to play a role in the growth of consciousness of all of us.'[4] In another piece the same year, he wrote of the 'Rabelaisian vitality and inexhaustible verve' of this work, noting that just when 'all western poetry is being consistently tuned to a minor key, Russian poetry is almost for the first time . . . becoming so exuberantly alive.' He found *The Ratcatcher* 'intensely Russian', the 'first really successful attempt (subconscious) to emancipate the language of Russian poetry from the tyranny of Greek, Latin and French syntax', and felt sure it was 'unlike anything that is associated with the appellation "Russian" in the mind of the English intellectual.'[5] If he was right, its destiny may perhaps be to change the consciousness of English readers as well.

In June 1926 Boris Pasternak wrote to Tsvetaeva from Russia, where he had stayed despite the Revolution. He had received a copy of *The Ratcatcher* from her and now gave it his full and excited praise: it was written 'in pure alcohol', was 'the very baring of poetry', 'no praise is high enough for the miracle that it is.' And it seems he too felt something like a 'growth of consciousness', for he wrote that had he not read this work he would have been more at ease in his 'path of compromise.'[6]

The Ratcatcher's oxymoronic subtitle, 'A lyrical satire', points to the presence of purely lyrical passages alongside bitingly satirical ones and also to the fact that its mockery is directed against everything in life which is emphatically non-lyrical. For this must be the angriest celebration of music ever written.

The writing of *The Ratcatcher*

The Ratcatcher is the last of the three long *poemy* which Tsvetaeva wrote – she also wrote eleven shorter ones. (The Russian word *poema* – '*po-èm-a*') – means a long verse narrative, often divided into parts). The two earlier ones, *The Tsar-Maiden* (*Tsar'-Devitsa*) of 1920 and *The Swain* (*Molodets*) of 1922, are based on Russian folk legends; *The Ratcatcher* is the only one of her poetic works based on a German legend. When she began writing it, in 1925, in Prague, having left Russia in 1922, she was still working on poems for the volume *After Russia* (*Posle Rossii*) (published Paris, 1928): her greatest lyrics and her greatest *poema* at once. Not long before this, she had finished two very fine works: 'Poem of the End' (*Poema kontsa*) and 'Poem of the Mountain' (*Poema gory*). So this was altogether a creative highpoint in her life. It was also a time of transition, of turning from shorter works to longer ones, many of them in prose. Before 1925 she had

published four short plays and twelve volumes of poetry. In the 1920s and
'30s, as well as more poetry, she wrote nearly fifty prose memoirs and
essays, many of them brilliant pieces.

According to her daughter Ariadna, it was when Tsvetaeva visited her
at her school, in 1924, in the small provincial Czech town Moravská
Třebová – neat, Germanic, prosperous and comfort-loving – that she
remembered the legend of the Ratcatcher of Hameln (known in England
as *The Pied Piper of Hamelin*) and thought of writing a version of it which
would be a satirical attack on the materialistic, unspiritual lifestyle repre-
sented by such a town. Ariadna further reports having heard her mother
say that Weimar without Goethe was Hamlin Town.[7] (For an explanation
of the spelling 'Hamlin' see the first note at the end of this book.)

Her version was also to engage with the Bolshevik revolution. Living
outside Russia, Tsvetaeva was free to say what she thought about that. But
what she thought is not easily summarisable. Married to a dreamer from a
revolutionary family, herself by temperament a rebel; always an enthusiast
for heroism; once papering her adolescent bedroom with portraits of
Napoleon; an admirer of all élan and aspiration: she held strongly to what
is known in Russian as *bytie* – true being, in which art, creativity and vision
belonged; it was the opposite of *byt* – dull, soul-destroying everyday
existence.

So there was much in her that sympathised with the ardour of the early
revolutionaries. In 1917-18, however, she did not hear 'the music of revo-
lution' which was heard by, for instance, the poet Alexander Blok; instead
her sympathies went to the losing side, the Whites. Her attitude to the Bol-
sheviks – and her inner political mood – may best be conveyed in her own
account of how, before leaving Moscow, she recited to Bolshevik audi-
ences, including Red soldiers, poems she had written in praise of the
White Army, and of how exhilarated she was to find them perceiving the
poems as being about them, the Reds. She quotes one of her listeners:
'None of this matters. You're a revolutionary poet all the same. You've got
our tempo.'[8] As Mirsky wrote: '. . . though an anti-Communist, Marina
Tsvetaeva is animated by a high and generous spirit of revolt that is hardly
in tune with the *émigré* feelings.'[9]

Legend and sources

In the summer of the year 1284 the German town of Hameln was so badly
overrun by rats that the Burgomaster promised a large sum of money to

anyone who would remove them. A colourfully dressed wandering Piper turned up and, by playing on his pipe, lured all the rats away and drowned them in the River Weser. But the reward was refused him and he went away angry, to return – some say at noon or at seven o'clock on 26 June – dressed as a hunter and with terrible face and strange red hat. This time, playing his pipe, he lured away all the town's 130 children over the age of four, together with the Burgomaster's grown-up daughter, and disappeared with them into the side of a mountain. Only two children survived: one blind and one dumb.

These are the main facts in the legend as told by the Brothers Grimm,[10] undoubtedly one of Tsvetaeva's sources. There have been many other versions of it, with minor variations. Tsvetaeva's chief divergences from the Grimm version are these: (i) the promised reward is the hand of the Burgomaster's daughter in marriage; (ii) the Ratcatcher is huntsman-like from the beginning (though without the terrible face); (iii) the children are drowned, with no survivors.

In Russian literature there is very little about this legend. Among other German treatments of the subject, Tsvetaeva certainly knew the poem 'The Ratcatcher' by Karl Simrock[11] which tells the whole story, Goethe's lyric poem 'The Ratcatcher'[12] and Heine's 'The Wandering Rats'.[13] She may also have known a prose version of it in Czech which was reprinted in Prague while she was there.[14]

In Simrock's seven-stanza poem the reward is marriage to the Burgomaster's daughter, and the children are drowned, as in Tsvetaeva's; other, more interesting, similarities are that Simrock insists on a miraculous or wonderful quality in the Piper (the word 'Wunder' is used four times), and that he makes the town council denounce music as at once frivolous and satanic. Moreover, the lines

| Er blickt so wild | He looks so wildly |
| Und singt so mild . . . | And sings so mildly . . . |

may have inspired her description of the Piper at the moment of the refused reward:

Lips smile.
Brows wild . . .

as well as the whole semi-demonic conception of this figure.

Goethe's three-stanza poem is a cheerful song sung by the wandering player who calls himself 'Ratcatcher', 'Childcatcher' and 'Maiden-catcher'. In addition to the tone of irresponsibility, these very words may echo in Tsvetaeva's 'Heartcatcher' (translated here as 'catcher of hearts') and in many other compound nouns.

Heine's fourteen-quatrain poem is the closest in spirit to Tsvetaeva's *poema*. Its light-heartedness is that of a poet obedient to metrics but to nothing else, ready to express his most furious thoughts provided they fit into firm and lively verse. The opening lines

Es gibt zwei Sorten Ratten,	There exist two sorts of rats,
Die hungrigen und satten . . .	Hungry ones and fed ones . . .

are paralleled in many ways in Tsvetaeva's *Ratcatcher*, as well as in other poems of hers. For Heine, while the well-fed stay at home, the hungry wander the world, 'ganz radikal, ganz rattenkahl' ('all radical, all ratty-bald' – word-play similar to hers) and are out for political upheaval. All they seriously want, however, opines the poet, is food. Tsvetaeva takes up this motif in a big way, but shows how music can convert the lust for food into a desire for Heaven or for world revolution or both. While she shares Heine's contempt for food-lusters, her main message is the power of music and poetry.

Browning's *The Pied Piper of Hamelin* has in common with Tsvetaeva's work verbal inventiveness, focus upon sounds, and many clever descriptions of wild movement. But it lacks the personal lyricism of Goethe's singer, the political grimness of Heine's rats and the satanic–miraculous hints given by Simrock, all of which were important to Tsvetaeva. The mood of Browning's poem is a harmless poking of fun, and it ends, most un-Tsvetaeva-like, with a moral teaching: Keep your promises. One Russian commentator writes: 'For the "unmasking" of the Ratcatcher, Robert Browning's common-sense and English sense of humour will be needed.'[15]

It seems a pity that some commentators apply the title 'The Pied Piper' to Tsvetaeva's work – in whose title, *Krysolov*, neither 'pied' nor 'piper' occurs – as it seriously confuses the question of who the main figure *is*. Certainly he is a Piper (and for simplicity I am calling him this in my Introduction, although in the text he is always 'the flautist' or 'the flute', only occasionally called a 'piper' by his detractors or, once, by himself) but, far from wearing 'pied' clothing, he is dressed from head to foot in green and is thus akin to a huntsman or man of the woods, not to a clown. 'The Pied Piper', moreover, inevitably brings Browning to mind, whereas Tsvetaeva probably did not know Browning's poem. She derived her story, as we have seen, from German sources, where the hero is always called 'the rat-catcher'.

Drafts of the *poema* (analysed by M.L. Bott[16]) show that Tsvetaeva had intended to weave another legend into it, the native Russian story of the town of Kitezh which saved itself from Tatar attack by sinking to the bottom of the lake on whose banks it stood. There it went on flourishing, and some hear its bells chiming to this day. The tale was a favourite of Symbolist poets of Tsvetaeva's time and she would have known Rimsky-Korsakov's opera based on it. Originally she planned a whole seventh chapter describing a life of eternal happiness underwater for the children and for Greta, the Burgomaster's daughter, married to the Piper. Though the idea was dropped, a few references to it remain, such as the title of Canto 6, 'Children's Paradise' – which, without the paradise, becomes quite mocking – and the instructions to 'bridesmaids' to prepare for the wedding.

In her memoir 'Mother and Music' Tsvetaeva mentions her childhood fondness for the French children's story *Sans famille* by Hector Malot.[17] This tells of a boy named Rémy (associated by Tsvetaeva with the sol-fa syllables *do-re-mi*) who is unkindly sold to a wandering musician (affirmatively named Vitalis); he comes to love him and, accompanied by a monkey and dogs, wanders all over France with him playing on a harp and singing. Though deprived of security, often ill, starving or in danger, he lives a clearly enviable life – of feeling and of proximity to nature and to art. Recollection of this tale may well have contributed to the creation of the Piper figure in *The Ratcatcher*.

A great deal of Russian literature lies behind, or works within, Tsvetaeva's *poema*. It has often been noted that she makes unusually full and vigorous use of literary tradition – quoting, evoking, and engaging in polemic with previous works. Verse satire has a long tradition in Russia; Tsvetaeva was inevitably conscious of Griboedov's great verse-comedy *Woe from Wit* (1825), Pushkin's satirical *poemy* such as *Count Nulin*, *The Little House in Kolomna*, *The Gabrieliad*, *Tsar Nikita and his Forty Daughters* (1820s) and of Nekrasov's long poem *Who can live well in Russia?* (1870s). Her mixing of styles – the serious with the frivolous, the fantastic with the realistic – is hardly her own invention. Prose satire has flourished in Russian literature too; more than one critic has spoken of Tsvetaeva's 'dead souls', implying a comparison between her Hamlin citizens and the Russian landowners in Gogol's novel of 1842. At the time when she was writing, there was much good satirical writing in Soviet Russia and we know that, unlike most émigrés, she kept in touch with what was being written 'over there'.

More particularly, as Yefim Etkind[18] has shown, she uses the rhythms, sometimes the words, from well known 1920s sailors' songs, from marching songs and from Proletkult[19] poems, and some passages show a close relation to contemporary poems by Vladimir Mayakovsky (1893-1930), one of the two prominent poets of her own time whose work echoes in *The Ratcatcher*. The 'I'-against-'we' discussion in Canto 5, for example, recalls Mayakovsky's defence of the 'I' and scorn for the Proletkult 'we' in part 2 of his long poem *The Fifth International*. And about Alexander Blok (1880-1921) Tsvetaeva had written a cycle of poems. Her praise for music and her sense that it meant infinitely more than performances in concert halls were akin to his. Amid the events and atmosphere of Revolution in January 1918, Blok had written an essay, *Intelligentsia and Revolution*, in which he challenged the Russian intelligentsia to 'listen to the Revolution', saying : 'We loved these dissonances, these roars, these ringings, these unexpected transitions . . . in the orchestra. But if we *really love* them and are not just tickling our nerves in a crowded theatre hall after dinner, we must listen to and love those sounds now that they are flying forth from the world orchestra . . .' 'For', he ends the essay, 'spirit is music.'

A recent study by Catherine Ciepiela[20] goes further than this and argues that Tsvetaeva's Piper leading the rats joyously and mysteriously to their perdition is a rewriting of the ending of Blok's famous poem *The Twelve* (finished immediately before the essay just quoted) where a phantom-like Christ figure leads twelve Red Guards into an ever thicker snowstorm. In answering Blok's 'Listen to the Revolution' with her own 'Trust in music', and in placing at the head of the marching rats (cf. Blok's Red Guards) the non-ideological, demonic figure that should rightly be there, Tsvetaeva, so Ciepiela writes, 'embraces Blok's view of the amoral, elemental nature of poetry more fully than he does himself.'

A considerable amount of German is used in *The Ratcatcher*. Some of it gives rise to clever puns, but what is interesting for an English reader is surely the way the German words and phrases fit naturally with the surrounding text, suggesting a liking for Germany, or at least for its language, which might seem at odds with the scorn being poured on the German townsfolk.

Tsvetaeva spoke German fluently from childhood and she loved German culture, especially literature, and especially the work of Hölderlin, Goethe, Heine and Rilke. Goethe is mentioned several times in this *poema*, and his *Faust* Part I (with heroine Gretchen) may be alluded to in the name Greta. A few years after *The Ratcatcher* Tsvetaeva wrote an incisive comparison (entitled 'Two Forest Kings'[21]) of Goethe's poem 'The Erlking' and Zhukovsky's well-known translation of it into Russian verse; her praise goes unhesitatingly to the original German poem for its refusal to prettify or evade, for its communication of the terror of the supernatural, and for its being, finally, what she calls 'more than art'.

At one stage Tsvetaeva planned to dedicate *The Ratcatcher* 'To my Germany', meaning German poetry, folktale and music. Another dedication she considered was 'To Heinrich Heine'. Close to Rilke with her otherworldly yearning, she was similarly close to Heine with her social angers and hatreds. Elements of her *poema* are heard, for example, in Heine's poem 'Anno 1829', from which she may have taken the idea of the *smell* of the burghers' lifestyle, and that of their valuing a good digestion, as well as, perhaps, the longing to escape from their narrow world into other lands *no matter where*; these lines, especially, sound like Tsvetaeva:

O, daß ich grosse Laster säh,	Oh that I might see great vices,
Verbrechen, blutig, kolossal, -	Crimes bloody and colossal, -
Nur diese satte Tugend nicht,	Just not this well-fed virtue,
Und zahlungsfähige Moral!	This morality always ready to pay!

In love with German culture and, as she confessed, with its *Schwärmerei* (visionary enthusiasm), while hostile to its materialism and *Spießbürgertum* (bourgeois philistinism), Tsvetaeva may appear to have put into the *poema* only her hostility, but in fact her love is expressed in it as well, since the Piper himself is German. Nor is she dealing in the commonplace contrast of settled rational Germans with nomadic mystical Russians, but she sets the two kinds of Germany (and thereby indeed two kinds of human being), the bourgeois and the artistic, in tension with each other, while any contrast with Russia is evoked either marginally (the rats come from Russia) or tacitly (she, the author, is a Russian – a fact she directly comments on in the text).

Story and themes

Summary

Canto 1 (191 lines) describes the inhabitants of Hamlin; Canto 2 (173 lines) looks into their dreams; Canto 3 (346 lines) depicts their market, the irruption into it of hordes of rats (who turn into revolutionaries) and the announcement of a reward for their removal; Canto 4 (561 lines) introduces the Piper: he entices the rats and leads them away to drown in a pond, pretending it is India; in Canto 5 (567 lines) the Town Councillors make speeches against music and reduce the reward from marriage with the Burgomaster's daughter to a papier-mâché flute-case; in Canto 6 (301 lines) the Piper lures the town's children away and drowns them.

CANTO 1: *Hamlin Town*

From the start the tone is ironic. These staid folk never sin and do not stay up to watch the comet (in a poem of 1923 Tsvetaeva had written: 'for the path of comets is the poet's path'). Caring only about food, money, rank and propriety, they have no 'soul' – and no music: the only references to music in this canto are to the absence of any clarinet in the town and to 'Schumanns' – a term of contempt. Beggars, too, are kept out of the town, and this will be recalled at the end of the last canto when the Piper is explicitly referred to as a 'beggar'.

At a number of places in the work the narrative (or dialogue, which soon takes over as vehicle of story-telling) is interrupted by a lyrical or satirical expatiation on a single topic: the first is here, in the form of an Ode to the Button. Buttons, descendants of the biblical fig-leaf, represent the desire to keep things contained and hidden, and are thus central to what Tsvetaeva has to say. This will be particularly explicit in Canto 5 when a flute-case is offered to a man who defines artists as haters of all wrappings.

Tsvetaeva thinks antithetically and makes this clear at the outset. There exist the satanic and the (all too) godly, the musical and the non-musical, the artist and the philistine, the naked and the overdressed, buttonless honesty and buttoned-up hypocrisy. 'God's children's buttons are all done up,/Those of the goat are not.'

CANTO 2: *The Dreams*

Having got the Hamliners to bed, the poet now spies into their dreams, proving that there is no sin or excitement there either. In his rich house 'stinking' of cleanliness the Burgomaster and his wife dream, like everyone else, of their boring everyday life. As if unable to stop herself, the poet imagines setting all this on fire, and the red of the 'red cockerel' (meaning fire) suggests Moscow with its red Kremlin walls, and 'red' revolution. We know from Canto 1 that no one in Hamlin thinks of arson and now poetry's easy entry into homes and dreams is likened to an invasion by fire; so poetry is allied both with revolution and with elemental danger. Greta, the Burgomaster's daughter, is an exception to the universal deadness of the imagination. Her dream-longings, which conclude the canto, mark the beginning of the subsidiary theme of her romance with the Rat-catcher.

CANTO 3: *The Affliction*

Rather more than a third of this canto develops the description of the town up to the arrival of the rats: its lively market and the gossip, which comes round to Greta again. A satirical ode in praise of 'measure', that is of the weighed-out, calculated, buttoned-up way of living, leads up to the lines '... overfill your sacks / With rice, the result's rats', at which a new mode and mood are abruptly introduced.

Like almost everything in the *poema*, the rats' entry is narrated through sounds: their pattering, trotting, rattling, hubbub ... and through the change in the sounds of the market – instead of separate voices a general roar delivers key words: 'Barns, stores!', and eventually: 'Rats! Groats!' The rats become proletarians seizing shops, museums, offices, lawbooks and bibles, making threats and gaining power, their behaviour conveyed solely through the shocked burghers' reports to one another on what is happening. Increasingly the focus is on language – 'We say "Brot", they call it "prod-"' – and we overhear White sympathisers giving in to their enemy by trying to pronounce one of the latter's main slogans, the word 'International'. The trotskyist hope of worldwide revolution will be an underlying fantasy-theme in the next canto where the seduced rats cherish the dream of extending the Revolution to India. But in Canto 3 there is still a realistic background, as the Comintern's plan for the international spread of Communism did at first focus on Germany where the year 1923 marked the end of a period of revolutionary upheaval.

Tsvetaeva has no compunction about switching from a German medieval scene to the imagery, language and happenings of twentieth-century Russia and, to some extent, Germany. With the same nonchalance she switches back, at the end of the canto, into medieval conditions, as the Town Herald strides through the streets calling out news of the infestation and of the Council's decree about a reward for anyone who gets rid of it. The inconspicuous concluding quatrain on the Piper's arrival is subtly managed: thus, the poet seems to say, may art enter ordinary life – quietly but dangerously.

CANTO 4: *The Abduction*

No sooner mentioned than close up, a song in our ears. The Piper sings as he walks. Singing and wandering are two modes unknown to Hamliners, and the walking is emphasised no less than the singing. As the children later, the rats are transformed by being set in movement no less than by being made to listen.

They are called to leave their fixed abodes and complicity with society's greed: clearly their position has changed since the previous canto. As the crowd of individual, often unconnected, voices comes to dominate again – with little or no linking narrative – a collective picture emerges of a situation in which, as rats, they have eaten their fill and grown fat, stopped hating cats, and feel their tails dropping off from inertia; while as men, they are now the ex-revolutionaries, as prosperous as the bourgeois they once ousted. Tsvetaeva certainly has in mind not just the setting up of the Soviet state but Lenin's introduction in 1921 of the New Economic Policy (the 'NEP') as a temporary aid to the country's economic recovery. This brought the return, until 1928, of private trading and of the pre-revolutionary contrast between desperately poor and ostentatiously wealthy (not unlike Russia today). Now, under the influence of the flute, the rats shed their NEP mentality and remember old slogans and battles. In the course of showing them pulled between energy and sloth, idealism and cynicism, Tsvetaeva mocks just about all the excuses people make for doing nothing. That their eventual resumption of activity and ideals is due to the passivity of being enchanted is part of what Canto 4 is about: the paradox of art's effect. It hypnotises, even paralyses, yet also inspires and liberates. Tsvetaeva undoubtedly knew Rilke's poem 'Archaic Torso of Apollo', in which quiet contemplation of beauty leads to the realisation: 'You must change your life.' So the rats are cast into a stuporous trance which issues in tremendous aspirations and a march to the strains of a battle song.

With its crazy procession – the impious crowd rejecting official society – and with the blurring of the boundary between animals and human beings, Canto 4 brings to mind Mikhail Bakhtin's discussion of 'carnival',[22] as do, in fact, other parts of the *poema*. For Tsvetaeva, however, liberation from restrictive forms, celebration of the splits and gaps in the conventional mappings of reality – these are not seasonal, or ritual, or partial; she argues for total spiritual change, and her carnivalesque crowd is not a chaotic one but moves in a single direction, led by a higher force.

There are several fine lyrical passages in this canto. One is the highly wrought piece starting 'Span-of-eye', a hymn to the horizon and the ocean. Another is the gentle song to 'Hindustan'; and, shortly after that, there is the remarkable 'poem' beginning 'How many years is the world?' This goes back through millennia to the first days of creation in a way that seems to have little to do with the story – wasn't it about fomenting socialist uprising in modern India? – but which alludes to the passage about Adam in Canto I. To be taken deep into art is to be taken back to before the original error, the eating of the apple followed by the putting on of the fig-leaf; back to the timelessness before creation. Pasternak, who was as much a Romantic as Tsvetaeva, wrote a lot about the ecstatic shift in the artist's consciousness whereby art originates; the rats are briefly initiates into this mystery – at the cost of their lives. Their drowning is preceded by an exchange between a sceptical 'old rat' – the only one not deluded (a sort of parallel to the one blind and one dumb child who survive in the Grimms' version) – and the musician, who stops his doubts with music and promises; it seems the old rat too goes to his death.

Later, Tsvetaeva wrote that the rhythms of *The Ratcatcher* were 'dictated by the rats' and the whole *poema* was 'written at the rats' command'.[23] Certainly the rats take up a surprising amount of the *poema* and are the most complex and protean figures in it. Not only are their many varied individual voices heard, but we see them collectively going through at least the following stages: rats; Bolsheviks; NEPmen/bourgeois; listeners to music and strugglers for self-renewal; world-revolutionaries; death-inebriates.

Meanwhile the Piper is not so much a developing figure as a diffuse and evocative one. In Canto 4 all his speeches are headed 'The Flute', as if he has merged into his instrument or into the very music. In Canto 6 the children will lose sight of him altogether as he becomes a vague music 'from sky or sea'. He is neither good nor bad – neither Pest-controller nor Murderer. In an essay, Tsvetaeva declared that she respected priest and doctor, nurse and nun, far more than any poet, who acts elementally (though *nothing*, she says, would make her prefer their vocation to her own). Consonant with her theory of elementality, the Piper is a force leading to death and at the same time a singer of genius. To the Councillors, of course, he will be just a man, one they despise and fear, but even for them he partakes of many traditions. He is gypsy, clown, trickster, wandering player, beggar and holy fool; he is also hunter, Green Man, Dionysus, the diabolical unknown. When outlining her planned characters, Tsvetaeva had jotted in her notebook: 'The Huntsman – Devil and Seducer – *Poetry*'.[24] (Tsvetaeva was, of course, not afraid of the Devil, whom she claimed to have seen in her childhood.)[25] Above all, the Ratcatcher is the Artist, with an aura of the divine. Indeed, God Himself is quoted, in Canto I, saying (in German) to the hiding Adam: 'Mensch, wo bist [du]?' *Mutatis mutandis*, this is Tsvetaeva's own appeal throughout the work: where are you, man, among the distractions, indulgences, disguises and clutter of your life? Can't you hear the music? Everything in *The Ratcatcher* radiates from this one high ambiguous value and points to the figure of the Ratcatcher who embodies it.

Canto 5: *In the Town Hall*

Pasternak thought Cantos 4 and 6, and the market part of Canto 3, the best; Canto 5 he liked the least: 'a tormenting chapter' taking us, he felt, away from our closeness to the Piper. It is true that the lyrical, until the very end, is absent from Canto 5. But it is surely as excellent a piece of writing as anything in the *poema*, a witty, angry, quasi-realistic piece cleverly placed between the two episodes of magical seduction. It is an exposition, and an exposure, of all the ways the unmusical think up to prevent any invasion of music into their lives. The theme is the place of art in ordinary life.

The speeches made against music are in three kinds of voice. First there is the philistine polyphony of Councillors declaring that no decent person could marry a musician – music is trivial and belongs at life's margins. Second is the voice of the Burgomaster, i.e. of political authority, which has to admit its enemy's power: music is fire, Furies, wild beasts, devils, revolt.

At this point something like Tsvetaeva's own voice states – in a 'poem' of its own – that in Hamlin there is no 'I', no experience of subjectivity, while for her there is *only* the 'I':

> I is an apple tree laden with fruit
> To the brim . . .

Strangely interrupting the dramatised narrative, this passage is her reminder that those whose opinions she is regaling us with have no conception of the reality of being.

The third voice is that of a Councillor known for his 'romanticism' and customary defence of the arts. Music, says he, insincerely, is ethereal, it is way above the ordinary mortal, and therefore cannot possibly be combined with everyday life. 'Marriage/Of Hamlin to genius would be as wrong/As a nightingale's to a cabbage'. The irony is, of course, that in Tsvetaeva's scheme of things he is quite right. The Piper cannot truly desire such a marriage, entailing as it would do a settled home and statesmanlike duties in the civic hierarchy; he can only desire to desire it (without the entailments) – after all, his passion is for the horizon. All the same, he is furious at the refusal to honour the pledge to him and his reply to the Council is Tsvetaeva's own credo. Thus the 'minstrel' (the artist) 'is the ripper of wrappers/ Off everything under the sky!' – and you should even, he says, 'Break all the flutes! It's in us/ Not in them, that sounds are sung.'

CANTO 6: *The Children's Paradise*

On a rough draft Tsvetaeva pencilled: 'Who will wake up the alarm-clock and free us from time?'[26] Her own dislike of mechanical time-counting was so great that she once said a major joy of her life was 'not to hear a metronome'. Into the ringing of the alarm-clock that wakes a child for school floats an unprecedented sound: the flute. Two opposed significances collide, and straight away it is the flute that wins. Once again everything is told through sounds – the music, the shouts of the children as they rush after it, their separate voices, the promises the flute seems to make.

Yet its Erlking-like enticements are, strangely enough, not univocal. For one thing, the Piper interrupts his attractive offerings with occasional hints at the children's actual watery destination: 'excellent places for rowing and fishing'; 'and – a bath for you all' . . . For another, still more unexpected, what he offers is emphatically divided as between girls and boys. For girls: dolls, thimbles, does, weddings, beads, passions, jewellery; for boys: guns, skittles, steeds, wars, bullets, games, flints. The distinction is particularly marked in 'Sounds for the girls and meanings for boys' ('sounds' being this poet's highest value) and still more in 'Pleasure for boys, and for girls – heavy care . . . /Joys for the boys, for the girls – despair': hardly designed to keep the girls following him! Why then do they follow him? In retrospect, most of what the Piper offers the children resembles in kind what they would have had if they had stayed at home, only more cunningly adapted to their taste: the materialism of toys and trinkets, and (to offer an interpretation of 'pleasure . . . despair') ordinary sexual relationships. Is this, then, all that they are able to want?

It is often supposed that Tsvetaeva sees the children as especially capable of freedom, even as her kin, potential poets. A sign of this could be their great immediate joy in breaking free of school and home, so different from the rats' slow, complex response (though the fact is that the rats are being induced to leave a life they were enjoying, which is not the case with the children); and Tsvetaeva certainly made remarks outside the *poema* which show a great respect for children's honesty and sense of loyalty. Within the *poema*, however, that initial love of freedom does not noticeably continue. An analysis of the twenty-four reasons the children give, one by one, as to why they are following the Piper – very like a collection of answers to a questionnaire – shows that eight are indeed the desire for romance, adventure or freedom, but as many as twelve amount to the mere wish to follow the crowd, while the other four are various uninspired reasons such as that they have forgotten to learn their lessons. Moreover, the last words spoken by the Piper to the children: 'don't think, just follow', while they could be kindly advice on how to listen to music, could also be read as cruelly sarcastic advice to the herd-minded. One might also ponder the almost luxuriating description of the drowning, with the water rising inch by inch over the children's heads. Overall, I think that Tsvetaeva is quite unsentimentally showing the children to be not much better than the rest of the Hamliners, even though we know they have been made that way by their parents and that their drowning is essentially a punishment of the parents.

Sounds/voices

'Of all the celebrated five senses I know only one: hearing,' wrote Marina Tsvetaeva in a letter in 1926, and in another the same year: 'Pasternak sees, in his poems, but I hear . . .' This theme recurs frequently in her essays. For example, in 'The Poet on the Critic' (also 1926),[27] writing about how she wrote poetry: 'I obey something which sounds in me . . . All my writing is careful listening.'

This emphasis on sheer hearing and on sound itself rather than upon music, say, or melody, is found frequently in *The Ratcatcher*. The very smell of the Burgomaster's house turns into a 'sound', resin is said to hum, school has a humming sound, and several times where we would expect the word 'music' we find instead the word 'sound': 'Who'd trust the dictionary, when there is sound, our priest and our lord?' says the Piper, countering the sceptical rat; the rats drown to the affirmation 'Seeing's dreaming! "I am" is "I hear!"'; the Councillors mock the Piper as 'mere sound': the children acclaim the flute with a cry of 'Sounds! Sounds!'

The *poema* not only distinguishes sound in this explicit way but is itself the most aural, audible, sound-based work imaginable. Even an unappreciative commentator in 1926, who found it 'nonsensical', admitted it was 'extremely musical nonsense'.[28] Rhythms, rhymes, intonations, assonances and alliterations – all are extraordinarily prominent, and meanings often derive from words obviously chosen for their sound. Pasternak wrote of the 'absolute, indivisible dominance of rhythm', praising especially the 'descriptive' rhythms used in Canto 3: with the entry of the rats 'the rhythm resembles what it is about – a very rare achievement. It seems to consist not of words but of rats, not of word-stresses but of grey spines.'[29] Everywhere, Pasternak writes, it is rhythm that 'calls into existence thoughts, images, turns of phrase and interweavings of theme.' The fundamental role of rhythm and the exceptionally wide variety of metres has been noted by all subsequent commentators, one of whom has calculated a 44 per cent presence of 'logoaedic' metres – that is, of lines which regularly repeat not just one metre (iambic, for example, or dactylic, with the usual variations) but – within one and the same line – two or more different metres.[30] This quite often produces a metre much favoured by Tsvetaeva, the choriamb ($-\smile\smile-$), and is seen in what the same writer has called 'the Hamlin strophe': a quatrain in which a line of two dactyls plus one-and-a-half trochees alternates with a line of a dactyl plus two trochees. In my English there is only, alas, an approximate reflection of it: 'Goggle-eyed schoolboys with unkempt hair/ Shaking their fists at Potsdam' – these lines from Canto 5 have this metre but more often my English reflects it less exactly, as in: 'Hymen's not meant for the lyrical poet -/ Even a child knows this./ Sobered-up nightingales, slow and sedate,/ Aren't supposed to exist' (also from Canto 5).

Another aspect of the 'sounding' nature of *The Ratcatcher* is of course something I have already referred to: the fact that almost all of the *poema* consists of speech. Voices predominate – in monologue, in dialogue, in hubbub; in dramatic exchange or in the type of 'deaf' conversation Ciepiela has aptly noted;[31] in rhetorical orations, in songs. There could scarcely be more 'heteroglossia' – to use the impressive word that has come to be accepted as a translation of Bakhtin's simple term *raznorechie* (varied speech). Yet at the same time the author's – also multiple – voice is never absent. When others speak (which is nearly always) we invariably know their relation to the author, who holds their voices suspended in her own voice.

In addition to her controlling of all the voices with her own silent one, there are at least four different ways in which the author speaks out audibly and personally. One is as narrator or 'implied author' in the few pieces of straight narration, as at the *poema*'s opening. Another is as lyricist, writer of poems, which are either to be taken as her own, as in the passage about 'I' in Canto 5 or – as it were – the Piper's, as in 'Hindustan'. A third is as modernist writer aware of writerly devices: thus – in Canto 1 – 'Pause for a rest here, reader', followed by a dialogue *with* the reader; the expressed intention 'not to wear rhymes out for nothing' (Canto 2); and a direct reference, in Canto 5, to herself as 'author, clairvoyant of lies'. This device is employed the most nakedly at the point in Canto 5 where briefly the entire clatter of the Councillors' voices is unceremoniously shoved into another perspective with the words 'And others' ideas aren't around in crowds/Either – there's only one:/The author's . . .'. The momentary total fracture of the fictional illusion reminds us that the work, and art altogether, is a pretence, like the Piper's pretence about 'India', at the same time as being deadly serious.

The fourth way in which Tsvetaeva's own voice sounds in the text is by its breaking into it as the biographical person behind the writer, making references to her own life-events or opinions. One such interruption, the interjection in the third stanza of Canto I – '*I* wouldn't touch him with a barge-pole!' – implies she is able to enter the fiction as one of its characters; another a few stanzas later, 'Lord preserve me from sleeping even/ Five years on one bed . . . ,' comes as if from a place right outside it. Then, still in Canto I, there is her perfectly eccentric, and one may well feel impermissible, allusion to her just-born son, 'my Russky'. These interruptions are made loudly and with gusto; the web of fiction is being hung as if concretely on hooks of real life.

Notes

In writing this Introduction I have been particularly helped by works in English by Simon Karlinsky, Michael Makin and Catherine Ciepela, for details of all of which see 'Further Reading'. I have also been helped by the following works in German: Introduction and commentary in *Krysolov, Der Rattenfänger*, edited, translated, and with commentaries by Marie-Luise Bott, with a glossary by Günther Wytrzens, *Wiener Slawistischer Almanach*, Sonderband 7, Vienna 1982; also by Marie-Luise Bott, 'Studien zu Marina Cvetaevas Poem

"Krysolov". Rattenfänger- und Kitež-Sage', *Wiener Slawistischer Almanach*, Sonderband 3, 1981, pp.87-112; and by Günther Wytrzens, 'Eine russische dichterische Gestaltung der Sage vom Hamelner Rattenfänger', Österreichische Akademie der Wissenschaften, *Sitzungsberichte*, vol.395, pp.5-42. Among works in Russian, those by Ye. Etkind, I. Malinkovich and T. Suni listed in the notes below have been particularly helpful.

1 Irina Ratushinskaya, preface ('Moya rodina') to *Stikhi/Poems/Poèmes*, Ann Arbor MI 1984, p.11

2 Joseph Brodsky, *Less Than One: Selected Essays*, Harmondsworth 1986, p.182

3 Pavel Antokolsky, 'Kniga Mariny Tsvetaevoy' [Marina Tsvetaeva's book], *Novyy mir* 4, 1966, p.218

4 D.S. Mirsky, review of *Krysolov* (*The Ratcatcher*), *Volya Rossii* 6/7, 1926, pp.99–102 (reprinted in 'M. Cvetaeva, Studien und Materialen', in *Wiener Slawistischer Almanach*, Sonderband 3, Vienna 1981, pp.266–9)

5 D.S. Mirsky, 'Marina Tsvetaeva', *New Statesman* XXVI/670, 27 February 1926, pp.611–13 (reprinted in D.S. Mirsky, *Uncollected Writings on Russian Literature*, ed. G.S. Smith, Berkeley CA 1989, pp.217–21)

6 *Letters 1926* (see 'Further Reading')

7 A. Efron, *Stranitsy vospominaniy* [Pages of reminiscences], Paris 1979, p.148

8 Marina Tsvetaeva, 'Poet i vremya' [The poet and time] (1932), in *Izbrannaya proza v dvukh tomakh*, vol.1, p.371 (see 'Further Reading')

9 D.S. Mirsky, 1989 (see note 5), pp.218-19

10 *The German Legends of the Brothers Grimm*, vol.I, edited by Donald Ward, London 1981 (legend no.245)

11 Karl Simrock, 'Der Rattenfänger' (c.1830), in *Ausgewählte Werke in 12 Bänden*, Leipzig 1907, vol.I, 1887, p.183

12 Johann Wolfgang von Goethe, 'Der Rattenfänger' (1803), in e.g. Weimarer Ausgabe, vol.I, 1887, p.183

13 Heinrich Heine, 'Die Wanderratten' (1855), in e.g. *Heines Werke in fünf Bänden*, vol.I, Berlin and Weimar, 1978, p.432

14 Viktor Dyk, *Krysař a jiná prosa* [The Ratcatcher and other prose], Prague 1923; doubtless Tsvetaeva also knew the version of the legend in *Des Knaben Wunderhorn*, the German folksong collection made by Achim von Arnim and Clemens Brentano and reprinted many times since its first appearance in 1806

15 Inessa Malinkovich, *Sud'ba starinnoy legendy* [The fate of an old legend], Moscow 1994, p.40

16 In the 1981 article cited in the introductory paragraph above

17 Translated as *Nobody's Boy* by Florence Crewe-Jones, New York 1916

18 Yefim Etkind, 'Fleytist i krysy (poema Mariny Tsvetaevoy "Krysolov" v kontekste nemetskoy narodnoy legendy i yeyo literaturnykh obrabotok)' [Marina Tsvetaeva's poem 'The Ratcatcher' in the context of the German folk legend and its literary treatments], in *Marina Tsvetaeva 1892–1992*, edited by S. Yelnitskaya and Ye. Etkind, Russian School of Norwich University, Northfield VT 1992

19 Abbreviation for Proletarskaya Kul'tura, the name of a cultural-educational organisation established in the Soviet Union in 1917 with the purpose of developing a distinctively proletarian literature and art

20 See 'Further Reading'

21 See 'Further Reading' under 'Translations of Tsvetaeva's prose'
22 See especially Mikhail Bakhtin, *Tvorchestvo Fransua Rable* (1965), translated by Helene Iswolsky as *Rabelais and his World*, Cambridge MA 1968, 1971, *passim*
23 Marina Tsvetaeva, 'Natalya Goncharova', in *Izbrannaya proza 1917–37 v dvukh tomakh* [Selected prose 1917–37 in two volumes], New York 1979, p.331
24 Marina Tsvetaeva, *Stikhotvoreniya i poemy v pyati tomakh* [Lyric and longer poems in five volumes], New York 1980-90, vol.3, pp.374–5
25 See, for example, her 1935 memoir 'The Devil' in Marina Tsvetaeva, *A Captive Spirit: Selected Prose*, edited and translated by J. Marin King, 1994, pp.188–203
26 As note 24
27 Marina Tsvetaeva, *Art in the Light of Conscience: Eight Essays on Poetry*, Bristol 1984, p.51
28 Mikhail Osorgin, *Poslednie novosti* [Latest news], 21 January 1926
29 Rainer Maria Rilke, Marina Tsvetaeva, Boris Pasternak, *Pis'ma 1926 goda* [Letters of the year 1926], Moscow 1990, p.155
30 Timo Suni, *Kompozitsiya 'Krysolova' i mifologizm Mariny Tsvetaevoy* [The composition of 'The Ratcatcher' and Marina Tsvetaeva's mythologism], Helsinki 1996
31 Catherine Ciepiela, 'Taking Monologism Seriously . . .', 1994, p.1021 (see 'Further Reading')

The Translation

I HAVE tried to convey as much as possible of the meaning in as natural-sounding English as possible, without obscuring the original's idiosyncrasy and strength, though much has inevitably been lost. Where I could, I reproduced the metre, or at least a semblance of it, and nearly always preserved line lengths. The *poema* is rigorously rhymed and I have used rhyme virtually throughout, without giving any priority to reproducing the rhyme *schemes*.

I will give a few examples of typical problems encountered.

The Piper tends to speak in ternary metres, characteristically (at any rate in Canto 4) in anapaests, and some of his most lyrical words are anapaestic; an example is the word *Indostan*. But whereas in Russian each word has a single strong stress, a three-syllable word in English readily acquires two stresses; 'Hindustan' has not the same rhythm as *Indostàn*. Nothing could be done about this. I merely tried to be anapaestic where I could.

Between the two opening stanzas of Canto I, which are strongly trochaic, and the fourth and fifth stanzas, which are equally strongly – almost incantatorily – dactylic, comes a vehement interruption not only semantic but also metrical (these two lines can be scanned as anapaestic with additional unstressed syllables at both ends). In English the interruption is still made but the metre has come out differently. So I hope I have given a sense of the rapid alternations of metres, even if not of the very same ones.

Russian is an inflected language and Tsvetaeva makes sharp use of the case-endings. In these lines in Canto 3 (repeated from Canto I) –

> Gorod gryadok
> Gammeln, nravov
> Dobrykh, skladov
> Polnykh . . .

which literally translate as:

> Town of plant-rows
> Hamlin, of morals
> Good, of storehouses
> Full . . .

a dense cluster of genitives rests upon a pair of nominatives ('Town' and 'Hamlin'), all of it contrasting with the next thirty-two lines (the 'Ode to Measure') where there is a remarkable near-absence of genitives. In my version:

> Rows of vegeta-
> bles, the morals
> Laudable, the
> Cellars full . . .

I have tried to replace the pulse and tautness of the original's pattern of endings, for which English has no equivalent, with a completely different pattern of word-ending sounds: ' –bles, -als, -ble, -ull'. Compensation of this kind also occurs here in my splitting a word over a line-ending, something the poet does not do at this point but does do, inimitably, elsewhere.

All the words in the first line of the *poema* – '*Star i daven gorod Gammeln*' – have English equivalents: 'Old and longstanding/is the/town Hamlin'; what cannot be found is an equivalent English form for the 'short form' of the two adjectives of the original, short forms being generally used in Russian for adjectives in the predicative position (often – and very much so in *The Ratcatcher* – suggesting more energy than the attributive long forms). Here Tsvetaeva exploits this grammatical peculiarity by employing a short form for an adjective that does not normally have one: '*daven*' for '*davniy*', thereby introducing a certain quaintness and a playful, faintly mocking element.

Occasionally the poet omits a word vital to the sense. 'Without your head than without your buttons,' she writes, supplying the absent word 'Better' in a most unorthodox footnote. 'Our Bible', she makes a citizen say, putting it in the accusative case but omitting the verb – I have imagined in the verb 'Gnawed'. At all such idiosyncratic omissions I have supplied the likely word.

Tsvetaeva is very prefix-conscious and will often present a concentrated variety of words all sharing one and the same prefix, as if to get to the last shred of meaning it can yield. In Cantos 3 and 4 a much repeated prefix (fitting the multiple motifs both of 'excess' and of 'change') is *pere* (pronounced as in 'peregrine' but not stressed) meaning 'trans-' or 'over-'; 'translation', for instance, is *perevod*. It was extremely difficult to preserve this kind of repetition in English, not least because the English *over-* kept acquiring a stress, thus becoming too noticeable.

My translation is not, then, except in some lucky passages, a 'literal' one, but it does represent an attempt to rearrange the text only where necessary (and there are many such necessities in any translation of poetry) and to convey the essence of Tsvetaeva.

Other translations

Krysolov has been translated in full into three other languages: into German by Marie-Luise Bott as *Der Rattenfänger*, 1982 (cited at the head of the notes to my Introduction); into Italian as *Accalappiatopi: Satirica lirica* by C. Graziadei, Rome 1983; and into Swedish as *Råttfångaren* by Annika Bäckström, Göteborg 1992. Excerpts from it have been translated into English by Elaine Feinstein (pp.74-80 of *Selected Poems*, 1981: see 'Further Reading'). I have been helped in the rendering of problematic words and phrases at numerous places by reference to the German translation and at several places by reference to the Swedish and the Italian ones.

The Text and Publication

Krysolov was first published in 1925-6 in six issues of *Volya Rossii*, a Russian émigré social-revolutionary periodical published in Prague. The readership of *Volya Rossii* was small. Tsvetaeva did not expect even the editors to like the work; she wrote to a friend: 'Poor Volya Rossii! Heroism against its will or "bonne mine au mauvais jeu." I'm convinced none of the editors has read it.' Few did read it, despite Mirsky's glowing review. Although until the mid-1920s it was possible for books published abroad to be sold in Russia, *The Ratcatcher* did not reach a Soviet public, and the sole published reference to it before the recent past was a negative remark by one D.A. Gorbov in 1927. (Pasternak's several pages of enthusiastic comment in letters, published of course only quite recently, stand out like the sun in a fog.)

As an émigrée Tsvetaeva could not be published in her own country for several decades. She began to be 'rehabilitated' in 1958, when some poems were published; the first extensive Soviet publication of her work was in 1965 when a large selection of her poems and *poemy* came out in the series 'Biblioteka poeta'. This included *Krysolov* but with the omission of more than 200 lines from Cantos 3 and 4, apparently to prevent the Soviet reader from associating the rats with the Bolsheviks. Prepublication of Cantos 1 and 2 in the journal *Novyy mir* was accompanied by praise of Tsvetaeva's anti-bourgeois stance. The volume was reviewed very positively in 1966 by Antokolsky.

Not until 1990 was the full text of *Krysolov* published in the Soviet Union. Meanwhile it appeared in the five-volume edition of her works in New York, the 'Russica' edition by Alexander Sumerkin, 1980-90. In the revised 'Biblioteka poeta' edition of 1990, published in Leningrad, of *Stikhotvoreniya i poemy* (Poems and *poemy*), edited by Ye. B. Korkina, the full text of *Krysolov* at last appeared in its author's own country. I have used this text. It includes the original subtitle and the two sub-headings in Canto 1, which were present in the *Volya Rossii* edition though removed by Tsvetaeva in manuscript in 1938–9. There have been several publications of the full text in Russia since 1990.

The Ratcatcher

A lyrical satire

Canto 1 Hamlin Town

Very old the town of Hamlin.
Meek in speech and strict in act.
Staunch in big as well as small things.
Splendid little town in fact.

When the Comet was predicted
Hamlin slept throughout the night.
Stoutly built, so clean and perfect:
Touchingly, it's rather like

(*I* wouldn't touch him with a barge-pole!)
Him – the mayor, the Burgomaster.

Tailoring isn't expensive in Hamlin:
There's only one manner of dressing.
Living isn't expensive in Hamlin,
And everyone dies with a blessing.

Tenpence a carcase; a jugful of cream –
Five; and cheeses, mostly,
Go for a penny. Just one, it would seem,
Of Hamlin's wares is costly:

Sin.

Inquire
Of some old sire:
'Dear means rare.'

No pretty girls letting down their hair,
No one in debt, and thirst

Never means more than a mug of beer.
Take gold or blood from your purse

If it's sin you're purchasing. Those who've slept
Five decades – fifty years! –
Together upon one bed (the dears)
Carry on sleeping. 'Sweat,

Decay: we've shared it.' Grass or mattress –
What's the difference?

(Lord preserve me from sleeping even
Five years on one bed – I'd as soon
Hire myself out as a pet dog's groom!)
Well, their souls are in Heaven.

 A thought, an epiphany:
What if
 They haven't any?

Hands – to squeeze sixpences out of pence,
Feet – just in case of a debtor.
But why have a soul? In what possible sense
Would a soul be anything better

Than futile things like a clarinet,
Or hammock, or basket of mignonette?

There isn't a single (write this down)
Clarinet in Hamlin.
There isn't a single soul to be found
There – but what bodies, upstanding

Solid ones! A concrete post
Is worth any amount of ghost.

They'll put on airs – then, gorgeous flowers,
To the ground! George, bow down!
'We, the burghers of Hamlin Town . . .' –
That has a proud sound!

Schoolboys, remember the ancient saw:
'Set eyes on Hamlin – and live no more!'

Juri and *Rührei* and *rühr uns nicht*
An (which means: don't touch us!) –
What a mélange. And their eyes so fixed
Downward? Not shame so much as

Thrift: keep looking and all of a sudden
You'll find a trouser button!

Pause for a rest here, reader. 'Lies,
Author, you're pulling wool over our eyes!
In this Eldorado, whose
Buttons would ever come loose?'

Beggars': – tramps all filthy and sodden,
Bringing diseases into the bedroom –

Vagrants': calamities thick and fast,
Life as a free ride!
No native beggars in Hamlin – just
One in the past, who died.

His skinny corpse was interred some way
Off from where paunchier corpses lay:

Thus did the Pastor in masterly manner
Decree – for not all deserve a hosanna.
The fat will never forgive the thin
One rag or trouser button. The thing

(He said) we have got to realise
Is that buttons should not be trivialised.

(A Short Diversion about the Button)

Button: holder up of the pattern
Of orderly living. Sober: buttoned.
Button! Shame of the primal Adam!
Death to underwear fashion and freedom.

Buttons to burghers: as tufts to Bulbas,
Or as the bellybutton to Buddha.

Into the mud – if you drop a button –
Go law and order. So, profligate,
Don't lose your button! It's all we've got
To redeem the error of ancient Adam,   ⋆

This figgish thing. For the leaf of yore
(*'Mensch, wo bist du ...?'*) was nothing more

Than the prototype (*'Bin nackt*: I'm bared,
Nothing on, that's why I'm scared') –
The very embryo and germ
Of a button: a button's platonic form!

This is the Button- (hear,
  Naked stomach!) idea:

It tells who belong to Satan's horde
And who are the sheep of the Lord:
For God's children's buttons are all done up,
While those of the goat are not.

If you're akin to an angel, man,
Button up as tight as you can.

Phantoms – aren't they? – looming by night,
Pouring out from Bedlams;
Beggars and rhymesters and genius-types,
Miscellaneous Schumanns,

Convicts ... There isn't the slightest doubt:
Better without your head than without

Your button. Sansculottes! Barefoots!
From Pugachov up to – Saint-Just?
For if a button's a trifle
What, gentlemen, is vital?

A button means for the State what a pound
Sterling means for the belly, firm ground

For the tree. When it's gone, you're exposed, it's
Mutiny! Looting! Murder!
Be very glad, then, mother,
If your babe has a button nose, it's

Proof of his goodness.
(Whereas my Russky
Is clearly hooknosed.

He's one of us, see.)

    ———————

A stop to this buttonesque nonsense, Muse!
Enough bobtailed truths!
Buttons won't save us from revolution:
They'll all tear loose!

If you're kin to a demon –
Bard, undo them!

    ———————

*(Here the Ode to the Button ends and the narrative is
resumed.)*

Rows of vegeta-
bles, the morals
Laudable, the cellars
Full –

For Hamlin Town is
Heavenly Town, it's

God's delight,
Brisk and bright,
Town of those who're
In the right . . .

For it's Heaven-Town,
        it's Haven-Town,
                it's Very-well-behaving-Town,
It's Buy-in-advance-and-take-care-Town,
                    it's Everyone's-getting-his-share-
                    Town.

No-guessing-Town:
Everything's clear.
Habit-Town, a blessing
Just to be there

In Heaven-Town,
That level town,

Loathed by the devil,
God's fond
Back-of-beyond . . .

A capital town for the Mayers and the Schmidts,
With everyone bowing to the powerful and rich.

Paradise.
Sweet as spice.
Not one person
Dreams of arson.
Abel-Town.
Such a stable town.

So you who're neither
Cold nor hot,
It's Go-there-Town
For you tepid lot –

To Ermine-Town
(No-vermine-Town),
Goodnight-Town,
Sleep-tight-Town.

First watch!
First watch!
End of the day – fasten the latch!
Is the cat let in? Is the dog let out?
First call on the night round.

Masters, unharness your serving-men!
Leisure, shake out your pipe's last spark!
Leave the lathe, working-men!
'*Morgen ist auch ein Tag.*'

Ten to ten!
Ten to ten!
Plug up your ears with cotton-wool!
Pile up your text-books ready for school!
If you intend to thrive,
Set the alarm for five.

Salesman, put away that chalk,
Housewife, put away that sock,
Turn back the sheet, it's dark:
'*Morgen ist auch ein Tag.*'

Ten o'clock!
Ten o'clock!
Not a whisper more!
Is the bolt drawn through? Is the key in the door?
Third call – as before.

Close the Bible, Father, come!
Tie, good wife, your bonnet on!
Husband, your nightcap onto your head!
'*Morgen ist auch ein . . .*'
                    Hark!
All Hamlin's gone to bed.

CANTO 2 The Dreams

In other towns (my kind of
Over-the-top-towns) –
Men dream of sirens,
Wives dream of Byrons,

Babies – of bogeys,
Housemaids – of horsemen . . .
Now come on, Morpheus,
In virtuous Hamlin -

What do they dream of?
Their brains aren't enormous:
A man sees his wife and
The wife sees her husband,

Their baby – the breast;
The fat-cheeked darling –
Her father's vest,
The one she's been darning.

Chefs dream of tasting,
Waiters – of waiting,
All as it should be,
Just as it should be.

Could knitting be neater?
No tangles at all!
Paul dreams of Peter,
And Peter – of Paul.

And naturally Grandpa
Sees grandsons (as scribblers

See commas), and maids –
Hearth and mistress.

Kaspar – precepts,
Pastor – pulpits.
Sleep isn't useless then?
Not just wasted time!

The dreams of the butcher
Are kilos of sausage,
Dreams of the pharmacist –
Scales, like the judge's.

The teacher's – a cane,
The upholsterer's – holland,
The dog's – a nice bone?
Wrong! It dreams of its collar.

Cook – a soup-tureen,
Laundress – a tub of steam.
All by the book.
All by the book.

And what of the Mayor?
He dreams of what's there.
Since he's the Burgo-
master, then ergo

He dreams of his burghers,
His well-behaved vassals.
A lord of the castle
Will dream of his servants.

Business – done.
Clothing – hung.
According to plan.
According to plan.

(My tone may be mocking.
And yet there's a virtue

In old things.) But not to
Wear rhymes out for nothing –

Let's invade, while he snores,
His monarchical mansion –
Solidly stanchioned,
It rightfully draws

Our attention . . .

———————

Without breaking the lock,
Without marking the sill . . .
In homes of the rich
What's first? The smell.

Intensive and tart,
Severe as the Torah,
Brash as a wart
On the nose of an actor.

All the flesh of matter
(Look – money-ledgers
Bound in best leather!),
All flesh's matter

Is in it, with festering
Gristle – no jesting!
No essence of things
But essence's thing-

ness is in this scent
With a whiplash sting –
No, no essence, the essent-
ial thingness of things.

No essence of anything
Ever ventured
In here! Rotting greens,
Old cellar stenches

Are better than this,
This reek of repleteness,
This odour of neatness
No one could miss.

Less a smell than a sound!
Sound of a wallet's
Clink – or gloved hand
Sliding down a red velvet

Stair-rail. You must
Understand: abundance
Stinks! – of complacence.
If also of dust –

Then not our poor kind:
Brought by the wind
And destined to vanish.
No, their dust's of damask

Drapes, with a whiff
Of items all sweet
From the laundry. And *if*
It should emanate sweat –

Then a prosperous sweat
Hallmarked by the State,
Not our kind (goat)
But banker-sweat, fat

From waistcoats: 'No giving!'

As far as the skies –
To you, O Hatred! –
A hundred-headed
Temple should rise

In the name of everyone living.

———————

Not touching the lock,
Not drawing the bolt . . .
(Have you noticed how locks
In dreams don't jolt?)

A dream is a lockless
Gate, a gateless
House, in dreams
People are shades,

Thieves . . .

Hundreds of brides to you!
All frills and furbelows!
No – obstacle!
Irres – ponsible!

Hour of the cavalier!
Break-ins! Burglings!
Send the red cockerel
To all snug dwellings!

To fat wives in wide beds
And their spouses so faithful.
That cockerel – as red
As the banners and citadels

In other cities . . .

Not touching the lock,
Come on, take a look
At the Burgomaster –
For no one's robuster –
At home in his castle.

———————

Homely is he, pink of cheek –
Burgomaster, sleepy-sleep.

Like a ticked-off week, unworried,
Is the Burgomaster's forehead.
What can he be dreaming of, then?
Nothing, absolutely nothing.

That's to say, he dreams (like trickling
Sweat from a heap of grease) of citizens.

Sleep on, Burgomaster's wife.
Sleep on, fatty, loyal for life,

Burgomistress, like a bird
With her craw filled full of food.
What's she dreaming, at her leisure?
He – of burghers, she (what pleasure

To yank her from her feather-bedding!),
She – of burghers' wives and weddings.

Some dream of their man gone missing,
 Others dream of Caesars kissing,
But a woman who's respectable
 Never dreams of what's delectable.

Hushaby, O Burgo-daughter,
Don't believe the things you ought to.

Wheat of Solomon her hair,
Like a river swift and fair.
What does this girl dream of, then?
What is she imagining?

Fragrances, whisperings . . .
More than that – everything!

CANTO 3 The Affliction

Gossips and gabblers,
Old wives, chatterers,
Mob-caps, shopping-bags –
Bábushkas, babblers.

'Herbs for the pharmacist!'
'Lard for the doctor!'
'Full-bodied red – just
Right for the pastor!'

'Straight from the milking!'
Butterbeaters, dairymaids.
'Extra-large wheat-grain!'
Meat-mincers, cook's maids.

'Health and happiness,
Strength for the season!'
'Fresh from the oxen –
Sinew for craftsmen!'

Gossippers, gabblers,
Bawlers, barrow-girls.
'Fleece-lined jackets!'
Mistresses, know-it-alls.

'Good clean tripe!'
'Cockerels – live!'
'Lovely and greasy!'
'Heart – for your sweetheart!'

'Cream! Thick and nice!'
Kindhearted neighbours.

'Fresh from the ice!'
Busybodies, rumourers.

'Come along! Check the weight!'
'Fry it! Won't shrink!'
'Goose-quills, strong and light,
Crying out for lawyer's ink!'

'Cabbage! – from the richest soil!'
'Conscience – for the judge's soul!'

Guinea-fowl, black-and-white,
Brides a-plenty over-ripe,
Stumpy little widows
Fresh from their pillows.

'Press, but don't squash!'
'Radish? Pure ruby!'
'Brains – for our boss!'
'With the bowl: half a ruble!'

'Like it? Then buy some!'
Bonnet-heads, skirt-hems.
Cooks – very finicky,
Chefs – with their ruddy cheeks.

Nose-flattening fingertip:
'Where's the most tasty bit?'
Palm held across the lip:
'Where's the most fatty bit?'

Catch a lot.
Show your zeal.
Fish it out.
Clinch a deal.

'Took the covers off the settee – '
'Having ever-so many guests!'
'Christening of the baker's baby!'
'News! News! The very best!'

Quiet and poisonous.
One eye glaucous.
Other eye oozes.
Coffee-boozers.

'. . . hankering for an older man!'
'*Just look* what she's got on!'
'Have you heard, the post-girl's got –'
'Have you heard?' 'What? What?'

Tittle-tattlers, tale-tellers,
'What? Her!' Muck-sellers.
'Wash your dirty linen . . .' Fibbers,
Slander-spreaders, chicory-bibbers.

'Green cravat, that's what he wore!'
'Lady-killer! Wants his way!'
'Swearing at his mother-in-law!'
'Things they say . . . down our way . . .'

'Special-ty . . .'
'Delica-cy . . .'
'Ha-ha-ha . . .'
'Hee-hee-hee . . .'

'And the Burgo's daughter Greta!'
'Barmy. And not getting better.'
'Hasn't slept for many a day!'
'What d'you say?' 'What d'you say?'

'Lights a lamp . . .'
'She'll be brought . . .'
'Full of hope . . .'
'With a bump . . .'

'And the linen in her dowry!'
'All alone! All alone!'
'Tells her dad she'll never marry.'
'Not a wife for anyone!'

'It's a sin . . .'
'She should be . . .'
'Ha-ha-ha . . .'
'Hee-hee-hee . . .'

'Look at her, just skin and bone . . .'
'All dried up, it seems to me!'
'Come and have a buttered scone!'
'Come to coffee, come to tea!'

So they close
The women's club.
Hotpot hissing
On the hob.

———————

Rows of vegeta-
bles, the morals
Laudable, the cellars
Full . . .

Measure! A holy call!
Over-proud – you'll fall.
Over-laugh – you'll weep.
Even a prince must keep

Favour and ire controlled:
Over-despotic? Revolt!
Over-sheepish? A fold!
Zuviel ist ungesund.

Measure! Moderation! Logic!
Over-eat – get colic.
(Over-scratch – a bald head.)
Over-fast and you're dead.

Over-keepfit – the plague.
Even go round the bend

Moderately – by the pound.
Zuviel ist ungesund.

Keep boldness under control!
The whip if you blame too much,
The same if you praise too much,
Don't give too much – that's all.

Don't overtop the top!
And see you control the amount
Of your moderation! Keep count.
Zuviel ist ungesund.

Measure! *Im rechten Mass!*
The keenest eye is outclassed.
Measure-by-eye and trust
Are long-dead ghosts from the past.

Foot-rule and measuring-tape
Are slogan and *Tugendbund*
For persons of grown-up age.
Zuviel ist un- . . .

Beauty's not all that's bad
In excess – d'you hear me, fat?

And – overfill your sacks
With rice: the result's rats.

Sago and salt and lard
Grant us with measure, Lord!
Over the market – roars:
'Barns, stores! . . .'

Weigh out your bounty, make it such
That it's neither too little nor too much.
Over the living fat go sounds:
'Stacks of it, mounds!'

To you, the greasy and mean –
A fat, oppressive scene:

Spite of the sated! Saliva
Spat from laden salvers!
But – here's the rub! – anger
Stems also from hunger.

Spite of those who don't eat:
Fed up – with no feed!
Never enrage the weak!
(Rats' pattering feet.)

Spite of those who aren't full:
Today you hear trotting,
Tomorrow – garotting.
(Rats trot down the street.)

(Spoken at a patter):

No sleep, not *satt*
(A rash of rats),
A leap at the fat
(A rush of rats).

House. Store.
They'll devour
Crumb and core
(Rattle of rats).

Stole in vain,
Stored in vain,
Raked in vain
(Gallop of rats).

HQ Hunger –
Rats' drum –
HQ Hubbub –
Rats' swarm.

Slit the sack:
Head Rat!

———————

They're over the bag and over the sack –
As over a corpse!
And a sound is rolling forth and back:
'Rats! Groats!'

Your tooth's turn,
Head Grain!

All your speech-making's led to this,
Workplace messiahs!
Over the live meat – a hiss:
'Rats! Supplies!'

(Your turn to flail,
Head Tail!)

———————

'Homage, they squeal, to the Head Glutton –'
'Grabbed the store, want us to pay! –'
'Stamping all night like a squadron –'
'And they say . . . down our way . . .'

'Zands! Flap-hats!'
'Posturing louts!'
'Sniffed through our cabinets,
Files and notes.'

'Homage, they squeal, to the Head Whoremaster!'
'The handful's grown to a host!'
'Serve, they squeal, the Burgomaster
Up on a plate with toast.'

Swarming
Whiskers,

Trouser
Buttons

Bitten!
'Schande!'
'Scandal!'
'Bandits!'

'Sure know how to grease their whiskers!'
'You say "Ow!" They say: "Hit!"'
'Gnawed our Bible – finger-thick the
Grease, they say, all over it!'

'Brazen! Filthy!'
'Saucy bastards!
Left their filth in
All our sauceboats!'

'Prayers, they squeal, aren't going to save you!'
'We say: "Gott", and they: "Leader!"'
'Dragged to bits our legal charter,
Every dot, rule and letter.'

'Dreadful manners!'
'Rags and tatters!'
'Shocking droppings
In the jam-bowls!'

'They'll gobble up the universe!
You say "Ham!" – they'll say "Shem . . .!"'
Twelve languages, they assert,
Are spoken by them.'

'Only two words reach us:
Comrade! And Cashbox!'

'They'll crunch up all the universe!'
'Subvert the sun!' 'Pervert the brain!'
'Came from some weird Russian place,
Landed here by ship, they claim.'

'Townsmen!
Unite!
Scandal!
It's a fight!'

'Give them one, they'll have a hundred!
No peace or sense of finance . . .
Eaten up the merchants' sugar –
Now they say they'll eat the merchants.'

'In addition,
All our hand-i-
llumined chroni-
cles are – pissed on.'

'Homage, they squeal, to the Head Hisser –'
'This is quite disgusting! Shame!'
'Yet they aren't entirely rat-like . . .'
'Are they only rats in name?'

'Bald patch!'
'Hair a thatch!'
'Who'd have said?
Wearing red!'

Very curious, most odd.
They go 'Devil!' if we say 'God'.

In a jump, to the spire's top!
'Have a heart!' – 'Shut your gob!'

We say 'Honour'. They say 'Rot!'
We say – 'Fetch!' They: 'Sit!'

We – 'Lower!' They: 'Higher!'
– 'Three!' – 'Fire!'

Bloodsucker if you're clad and shod,
Parasite if you're not down in the mud.

'And their language!'
'And their language!'
'And their language!'
'And their language!'

We say 'Brot', they call it 'prod' –
The tongue can't get around it!
We thought he'd croaked: he's up, by God –
Arsenic's confounded.

We say 'rob', they call it 'kom –'
We – 'mob', they – 'intern':
Devil's Commissars of Scorn –
Devkomdung: splits your tongue!

This is it, the new-made world!
Didn't sweat – you shan't eat,
Didn't pant – you shan't eat,
Decent sort – you shan't eat.

Up till now you're in one piece:
Didn't sweat – you'll be shot,
Didn't join us – you'll be shot,
Decent sort – you'll be shot.

(In legal tones: the accusation):
Of thievery.
Of nepotry.
Of rascalry.
Of sorcery.

(In conspiratorial tones):
Aren't we all White?
That's right.
So what's it about?
One word.

'It covers the world!'
'With a cover of gold!'

'It builds to the skies.'
'It bears a high price.'

'It's that sort of word!'
'It's that sort of word!'
'It's that sort of word!'
'It's that sort of word!'

(Trying to pronounce it):
Inter – gnash.
Inter – gnaw.
Inter – val.
Inte – gral.

Smash 'em all.
Trash 'em all.
In – ter –
Nash – er . . .

———————

No more of these legends!
Hark to the Herald!
Sons of the Fatherland –
Hearken and understand!

Never mind detail:
Hamlin's in peril!
In hills and in dells –
Hear what the Herald tells!

Everyone, one and all,
Listen what may befall:

All of our property,
Fame, class, prosperity –

Hangs by a fraying hair!
Citizens, hear!

Hear the decree – so intelligently
Decreed by the Council, our maid of good counsel:

'Whoever – though yid
Or devil – can rid
Our town of its rats
Shall have as reward
To be Mayor's son, that's

To say: son-in-law,
Meaning: marry his daugh-

(A roll on a drum . . .) –
ter. In Hamlin the um-

pteenth year of the Lord.'

———————

That very moment – blame the sentry,
Why didn't he warn that a stranger was seen? –
Into the town a man made his entry,
Carrying a flute, dressed all in green.

Canto 4 The Abduction

Tra-la-la . . .
Over Germany near and far . . .
Tra-la-lee . . .
Over garden, pasture and lea,
Over cities charming and clean . . .

Here I go,
Giving praises to Music – my Queen.

Here today
(Only half of me, never the whole) . . .
Tra-la-lay . . .
But tomorrow I'm far away –
So let everyone slander and scold,

For there's nobody, old or young,
Who can hear my song
Without turning a yearning eye
As I wander by.

To the other side of all fences! –
'Catcher of hearts!' –
To where you are new and your senses
Have never been fathomed or parsed.

'We've got used to this life!' they chime.
Do you call that life? It's slime!

On the road!
Come on out of your fixed abode!
Cross a bridge!
Come on down from your settled ledge!

Says the Piper: To hell with your prudence!
Migrate!
Does a peacock enumerate
The hues of its iridescence?

Hey-di-ho!
Now to hell with you, measures of dough!
Hey-di-how!
Split open, sackfuls of flour!

No more of Hamlinish (fluters aren't farmers)
Barley and timber –
Step over –
To the pearls and palmtrees of India.

With a trill!
Why be storemen? Be human, instead!
Overspill!
Why be doormats or snails? Stride ahead!
Here's Hamlin but there – Himalayas,
Heavenly spheres.

They're at sixes and sevens –
It's mud and they're calling it Heaven.

On your feet!
There are holly trees all down the lanes.
Make the break!
Those are barberries in the ravines:
Sour and sweet.

To be sated!
This shameful desire they call sacred.

On the move, rats!
Have no truck with satiety!
On the hoof, rats!
Away from the greed of society!

It'll have your sword!
                    . . . I'm attacked by a word:
'Ratcatcher? Rat-courter!
Caught them – you court them!'

Rats, get –

'What's happening?'
'What's this, then?'
'It's sickening!'
'It's nasty!'

'It's tasty!'
'What mystery?'
'Unseemly!'
'Truth is we're fed up. Extremely.'

'Mankind cannot live without struggle!'
'My stomach is simply enormous,
It's getting to knee-length – regal.'
'Mine too – it's truly pendulous.'

'Mankind can't survive without battle!'
'My waistcoat and paunch – I'm appalled –
Are parting: it's more than a quarrel.'
'Same with me – I'm going bald!'

'Who'd be a saint?'
'Can't gnaw any more!'
'Not a trek – a treat!'
'Can't thieve any more!'

'Two croissants for breakfast.'
'I'm plagued with deafness.'
'I'm becoming toothless.'
'I've lost my toothlust.'

'To put on my shoes I must lean
On my servant . . .' 'A High Road –'
'Without struggle the widest ravine
Is jail.' 'Unshod, then! Good!'

'A grave, not a march.'
'My tail's going soft.'
'Three dumplings for lunch.'
'Mine's fallen off.'

'No malice, peace . . .'
'Our bellies increase . . .'
'No sooner dressed than it's dinner once more,
Three courses or four . . .'

'We'd have run a mile if we'd understood . . .'
'Do you still remember the bashlyk hood?'

Thrust, grab,
Joust, stab.

'To put on my jacket I need
A servant . . .' 'High, indeed –'
'In that land where we strode so bold and quick,
I was known as a Bolsh- . . .'

'Pass. I can do no more.'
'My eyesight's all of a blur.'
'My style has turned impure.'
'My brain's clogged up with fur,
Murky . . .'

'To Karlsbad!' 'To Moscow!'
'My bum's drooping down.'
'Each morning – lumbago.'
'Mine's down to the ground,
Nearly touching . . .'

Get skis and – to Heaven!
'My rupture!'
'My heartburn!'

Once you're
Used to
Feasts, you're
Done for.

'Three days like this and I'm finished.'
'I've been getting a fondness for cats
And salesmen.'
                              ' ... no longer bothered by slaps.'
'My daughter has got to be christened:

Means nothing to me, but it should
Do her some good.'

'Not a rest – a nest!'
'I'm losing my zest . . .'

FLUTE:
Somewhere – Ind- . . .

'I'm getting enamoured of *vint*.'

'Making sure what's mine and what's yours.'
'Locking the linen . . .'
  'How he ran for his life!'
'Putting starch in

My washing.'
'And I'm personally waxing the floors.'
'My aversion:
I can't abide any shade

Of red.' 'We're the same!'
'I nod off at seven from shame.'
'That was really a raid!'
'I find I'm afraid

Of shadowy places . . .'
'Of motherly glances . . .'
'Of the masses . . .' 'I've qualms
About guns . . .' 'And why are there coats of arms

For nobles? And nothing for us . . .

Brushed out,
As if mopped!'
'And the bribes!'
'And the gout!'

'Back to the hold!'
'Where the thunder rolled!'
'. . . Oh we strolled –'
'. . . teeth full of gold.'

Into the midst of the hail and the gale!

FLUTE:
O–ver–fed.

'I just throw it all up again.'
'Diagrams, graphs – well of course
They make you rush to the stores!'

' "Kamerad" is old hat
Now we're grey-haired and fat.
I suggest we transfer
To "Mister" or "Sir". . .

For . . . form's sake. Listen:
"Good Sir, Master Citizen." '

FLUTE, *insistent:*
Overfed.

Overslept.
Enough to eat – you'd never
Have come. Nor ever
Have managed a mile – not one third,
Had you slept the sleep of the dead.

Overstayed.
Overstaid.

To work miracles, don't sit down.
An old tune.

Over-sat.
Come on out of your comfortable flat!
Overturn your home!
Go far!
Don't grieve for the walls you warmed!
Nor for fallen stars!

Peace – to the dead.
Come out – into life
Down this very path where I've led

You – a bit to the left.
'My sons – all fifty –
They've all come top!'
'My musket's rusty.'

'So what, there are plenty
Lying in the ditches!'
'From our barnyard niches
 To India?! Pell-mell?'
'Yet we took

Perekop!
Did we look
For a well-trodden track
To Moscow?' 'To hell

With the past and its lindens
Three hundred years old!'
'We're setting out bold-
ly to overthrow India!

We'll storm our way through!'
'But I'm building my house!'
'We're building a world!'
'But I'm gnawing my cheese!'

'You can't overspit your own nose!'

FLUTE:
Overspit!
Into the blue! Into June!
Into newness!
And look – a new moon!

To stride like a hero,
Your clothes must be zero!

To belt up your coat –
Not a single oat!

The regiment! Glory!
A clinking of ivory.

No more groats with sugar!
Grope again at the trigger.

. . . with oil . . . with lard . . .
Long live the red . . .

Rats! March ahead!

Sick and tired of home-made stuffing!
Three centuries old – it's atrophied!
Stale! Catastrophe! Now nothing
Stops us! Gnash your teeth, your rat-trophies! –

Sick and tired of milky puddings!
Something hotter's in our knapsacks!
Three billion Pacific-Ocean
Rats stare from afar in rat-packs –

Feverish, swarming, a
Rats' *Sturm und Drang*!
Battles with musk-deer on
Shores of the Gang-

ès! No time for cake or sausage,
Hamlinish, Viennese or Pragueish!

Raid the cosmos! The world's against us!
Courage, rats who haven't rotted!

'Tasty pastries!'
'Don't stop!'

'Lovely lardcakes!'
'Snarl at the lot!'

Not a crumb's to be stowed away –
Past the Town Hall – quick march!

Swagger! Chests out! Don't sway!
Past the market, past the church.

Like a thought – a message – a shot – a passion –
Past the Burgomaster's mansion.

But – on the balcony . . .
Ah – from the balcony . . .
A sort of glowing . . .
A sort of bowing . . .

Trace of Shiraz,
Pink cheeks a-blush . . .
And the Piper – hush –
Has he picked up a rose?

(Only a courtesy!)
Don't hold back!

If you're after ecstasy
Don't look back!

See: with its brows
Against space, the last house.

———————

Span-of-eye!
To the verge, to the edge of the sky!
'But we're slow, we'll never clap eyes on . . .'
Aha! – a rhyme for 'horizon'!

Fleet of foot
Runs the fleet in its seventy-league boot,
Overtaking us once and for aye,
Far beyond any brow, any eye:

Cook of dreams!
He is melting the 'is' with the 'seems'.
So wax flows –
Far beyond all our yearnings and woes!

Yearning-gauge!
Just as blue upon blue – carry eight –
Gives the speed (like script on a slate)
And the measure – of yearning and rage.

Pluck-an-eye!
Not in vain do they tell in Siberia
Of an ogre
Who sucks out your children's eyes.

Not in vain
The passionate female hysteria
Of hordes and of clans
For one who can swallow the mysteries.

Tug-of-eye!
Eye-wrencher and breaker of eyes!
Oh the blue
Sea-blue of your eye, span-of-eye!

Going out in the breeze –
You should talk to the orderly cranes.
Into corn of the east
Ask the convicts with blue-blooded names.

'Him!' 'And beyond?'
'It's still him!' 'But – beyond him?' 'It's still . . .'
'Heart's desire!'
I can't bear to be here.
Take me far away, far

Beyond the horizon! . . .

————————

'Dreaming it all?'
'Lull or a squall?'
'Russet or grey?'
'Going which way?'

'Wrong sights!'
'Wrong heights!'
'Wrong trees!'
'Wrong breeze!'

'Other world? Or ours?'
'Have we walked for hours?'
'Three years? Or one?'
'How far have we gone?'

'Wrong views!'
'Wrong blues!'
'Wrong dusk!'
'Wrong dust!'

'Did I run? Or sail?'
'Hamlin? Some district . . .'
'Hamlin? Missed it . . .'
'Hamlin? A tale

Was told about it.' 'An old one at that:
Left of Hanover on the map.'

'Wrong woods!'
'Wrong bush!'

'Wrong chirps!'
'Wrong thrush!'

'Young as a Greek!'
'Hamlin? A place
For tourists.' 'No trace.'
'Hamlin? Oblique–

ly I read of it once while my aunties were sewing . . .'
'For me, Hamburg's enough to be going
On with . . .'

'Wrong breath!'
'Wrong gait!'
'Wrong laugh!'
'Wrong light!'

Not white – blue . . .
'Hamlin? A blank!'
'Hamlin? I think
It's a kind of food –

Remember: we once had a beer and ate an
Appetising *Hammelbraten* – ?

A delicious piece!'
'Hamlin? Don't tease . . .'
'What Hamlin? Please!'
'Hamlin? Bees

In the brain!'
          'I insist:
Hamlin – doesn't exist.'

Dust.
Rust.
Mort.
Nought.

Our salt – bullet dust!
Hole in a sack – that's our past!
Worse than the plague,
Yet – salt of the earth!

Our blood – black as pitch!
Wipe off blood – with blood!
Brains may complain –
Yet we're blood of the earth!

Roll of drums – that's our trill!
'Slave! Aim left to kill!'
Lower than earth,
Yet we're flowers of . . .

'I tell you: those are the wrong hills!'

'This isn't Germany!'
'Much longer haul!'
'Not – Germany!'
'Not – Gaul!'

'Stoned – and how!'
'Just say "Wow"!'
'Not Germania!'
'Not Romania!'

 'Quieter than quiet!'
'Longer than long!
Scythia? – Wrong,
Must be . . .'
                    'India!'

FLUTE:
Hindustan,
To the verge, to the land of lands,
Like a blue tun
Is your nightsky, Hindustan.

You have turned
'Here' to 'there', and we give, not gain,
Scale of scales
Climbing up to the temple's crown.

Rice and corn
Being carefully rinsed from the urn
In a girl's arm –
Your quietness, Hindustan.

As a hunter returns
From forest lairs and alarms
To his bed of down –
To your quietness, Hindustan,

Comes a man . . .

––––––––––

'I see pagoda domes!'
'I see a blue-blue shine!'
'I see rice-paddies!'
'We're going to drink palm wine!'

Since the primeval thunder,
Since the primeval slumber,
Rats and children have craved
Candy and sugar-cane.

How many years is the world?
How many moments old?
Capsicum blooms in the winds.
In the winds, sugar resounds.

Shagreen – not virgin soil!
In the blue light a trawl
Of plum. It's the fourth day
And no countable year at all.

Resins'
Humming.
Hinny.
Oxen.

No canvas, but a carnage
Of colours. Primal silt.
Proto-creative scrawl
Of genius. First trial

Of demon strength. Flint
Struck by the first tool.
Fourth hour of the world,
And no countable day at all.

Ganges'
Maids!
Mango
Shade!

Indigo ! First tint.
India! First plaint
Of animal. Look – the world,
Poet, is four moments old!

Foretasting when I'll fold
 Time like a rough draft . . .
A flash of the eye, the last,
And the world's not a moment old . . .

OLD RAT:
Something's nagging me! As though –
Isn't it – somehow – almost . . . This
Region resembles a place I know.
Surely that pagoda is

Our old cornbin . . .
                              'Turbans! Brahmins!'

OLD RAT:
Call this India? Those are barns,
Barns and not . . .
                              'Bazaars! Bombay!
Dervish! Cobra!'

OLD RAT:
                              No, it's hay,
Haylofts . . .
                              'Rajahs' domes to the sky!'

OLD RAT:
Tropics – in a field of rye?!

In words of one syllable, black and white:
Not bamboo. More like a turn-pike.
Those are mills, not palm-trees.
Kites, not condors. Not maize, but peas.

And we're not a regiment, we're just a handful –
And we've only gone four miles from Hamlin!

FLUTE:
Load of lies!
Smash the egoist, stop his yarn!
Squinty eyes,
To take an elephant for a barn
And its trunk for his own nose!
For such an idiot, anything goes.

(Fiercer! More of it! Spread it! Rise
Up the chromatic scale of lies!)

Liar! Worse!
To see the future as your own arse!
Dead and stinking
If all you see is your rear as you pass
And in open space you're forever thinking
Of places to stop. Perverse!

Distorted!
Put your trust in Music:
It'll lead you through granite,
For dynamite is
Less old than Music . . .
                    'All – united!
To the horizon!'

'Lake!'
'Turquoise!'
'Pink
Sweep of . . .'
'See?'
'Oh if . . .!'
'Ibis!'
'Flamingo!'

OLD RAT:
That blue
Will drown you!

'Tropical mirror!
Softness
Of sapphire!
Lotus!
Papyrus!'

And so they enter
Their bedroom of water.
Palmtrees lean
Low to the lake.
'We'll be clean!
We can slake

Our thirst on lotus juice at our ease:
Peace.'

FLUTE:
A watering-place
For all the displaced,

With lodging and food
In plenitude.

OLD RAT:
But it's Hamlin pond – unblock your ears!
It's been rotting there for three hundred years
And the smell is vile!

FLUTE:
A cro-co-dile!

'O blessed view!'
'It's coming true!'

OLD RAT:
Swill!
Bilge!

'Glimmer of silk!'

OLD RAT:
Tadpoles!
Headless fools with your headman: just
Tadpoles – nothing more at all!

FLUTE:
Who'll trust
A dictionary (all it can do is hoard
Definitions,
Work of technicians),
When there is sound, our priest and lord?

OLD RAT:
I tell you, this man's a liar!
A liar, an agent!

FLUTE:
It's not music that lies, but the instrument.

OLD RAT:
Trug und Schand!

FLUTE:
Not music that lies, but its maker.
Note the difference!

OLD RAT:
This is a swamp! We're walking on twigs!

FLUTE:
Rather music than arsenic.

OLD RAT:
Death!

FLUTE:
       So what?
Better a lake than a silo's peril.
Better to sink than to rot.
Slime? Nonsense! Coral! Beryl!
Emerald . . .
       And they'll perish soon
Not in a puddle but in a tune!

What is the body? A shadow's quiver.
Body's span? A spume, a shiver.
Here's Nirvana – its very sap.
A palm trunk? A shaft for a flag.

Into a world of rainbow curves
Sound will be our guiding pole.
Two arms aren't enough to serve.
 Sound is the pole, the flag – your soul.

Seeing's dreaming! 'I am' is 'I hear!'
The tone goes lower, the meaning higher.
Here's the lowest. The body's splash.
And – the note of notes: shshshsh.

The air is stifling. The water's fresh.
Somewhere each of us is a tsar.
(Yes, in death . . .)
                    Eyes peacefully closed . . .

In this India *we*'re the rajahs.

———————

Rajah on rajah!
But those rats are
Utterly gone.
Rings on a pond.

CANTO 5 In the Town Hall

'Greetings, Councillors –
Privy and State!
Ancient Hamlin's
Relieved at last
Of its freebooting guests!

Roasting-pans, celebrate –
Kettles, resound –
The rats are drowned!

 Beat on your pans
Till the alleyways ring!
"I'd be a cook
If I weren't a king!"

Council, rejoice!
No more troubles and fears!
Every warehouse
Purged of predators,
Every head – of ideas.

Beat on your frying-pans!

Deck out the streets,
Indulge in your sweets –
Your sugar with chicory –
For this grand victory
Without fists or bullets,

A party for pots and skillets!
Behold the day:
The rats are away.

Like it or not –
Everything's done, you see:
What you desired you've got.
Now – what you promised me.'

A whisper,
A stir,
They glance
Askance,

And with poppy-red cheek
And with eyebrow oblique:
'What's that you say?'
'When, in what way?'

(Shelves of clay pups
In a pottery shop.)
'What does he mean?
What's this we're seeing?'

'No whats or wheres! It's clear, in fine,
The girl named Greta is now to be mine.'

'Greta? But this is Germany!
There's as many Gretas around as Hanses!
There's hardly a girl with another name
In Hamlin's streets and manses.

Looking for Greta in Hamlin's as simple
As going to the sea-shore to look for a pebble.
It's a kind of contredanse:
First a Greta, then a Hans.

Oh, you'll get your
Promised Greta!
Fair and buxom –
Dozens of them!

Assuming you're not blind or lame
You'll find a Greta – they're all the same:

Identical dimples,
Identical pimples –

Such dear little creatures,
With similar features.

Now whose Greta is it
You'd like to visit?'

'You're joking! Who was I whistling to get
If it wasn't the Burgomaster's Gret?'

Shift of feet.
Nervous tic.
Worried bleat.
Hiccups: hic!

Councillors flutter.
'Tish!' – they sneeze.
'Him a suitor?'
'If you please!'

A hundred pigs have begun to snort.
Their bellies quiver with every grunt.

'What a laugh! What a scream!'
Bald patches begin to gleam.

'What, our young maid in her
Dainty pinafore?'
'Yes, indeed.' 'With her
Basket of honours?'
'Her, of course.'

Councillors snort,
Twist and contort.
'What a fop!'
'Thinks he's top!'

Narrowed glance.
Cheeks – puce.
'Hans the Gans!'
'What a goose!'

'Our young lady with basket of gold?'
                    'As you have sowed . . .'
'Our treasure and treat,
Our field of wheat?'
                    '. . . so shall you reap!'

'That music bag!
Dressed in rags!'
'As a son-in-law!'
'As husband for . . .!'

Very sly!
Very fly!
The Burgomaster
Neighs with laughter.

'So – a quick wedding?'
                    'Council!'

'The town's first maiden?'
                    'Scoundrels!'

' "Devil, mad, blind or yid,
Anyone who can rid
Hamlin of murine pests,
He shall be one of our best,
Highest in town and castle:
Son to the Burgomaster . . ."'

'Stop!
This isn't a rustic hop!
Will you pipe your tunes at our Council?
Less fast! Andante! I do recall
Something was said of Jew and devil,
But of "music-makers" – nothing at all!

Oh, after the service it's "Come inside,
Friend, with your piping and fiddling" –
Of course musicians are welcome at weddings:
Just not at the side of the bride!

Marry a piper? A semi-quaver!
Mere sound! A reed with incisions!
It's unheard-of! Who would ever
Get married to a musician?

What? A piper? A bag of nerves!
My daughter? Sooner a blacksmith!
What would she do with his fifths and thirds
In the matrimonial blankets?

Marry a piper? A naked bean!
In England perhaps – but listen:
In Hamlin it's never been heard or seen
That our people marry musicians.'

'What is music? Twitter of birds!
Pastime! A children's plaything!'
'What is music? Noise in your ears.'
'Jollying up for a wedding.'

'Inconsequential scrape of strings.'
'Shouts of "Bravo!" Anguish.'
'Music? It isn't even the goose,
It's merely the goose's garnish.'

'Mustn't forget that when I was young
I too was one of the lads!'
'Just a piece of wood and some feline gut,
Combined with a certain knack.'

'Scatters your wits! A narcotic fume!'
'No, when we hire a singer,
It's so they'll sing us a soothing tune
To help digest our dinner.'

'With women around, and a tankard of beer,
It's pleasant to have a song . . .
A tune or two before turning in . . .
Though it mustn't last too long.'

'What is music? Soon as it starts –
I'm dying for it to stop!'
'Me, I'm different – I like the arts,
But loud, please, with a lot

Of bass . . .'
                    'See, I've got eight little mites
And I'm up at dawn to feed them . . .'
'It's an infringement of citizens' rights:
Can't hear yourself speak in that bedlam!'

'Music? Boring . . .'
'A nuisance, a yawn!'
'Waffle! Padding!'
'Pure decoration . . .'
'Nothing at all, with modulations . . .'
'After the meat, the pudding.'

'You've got it wrong, sir –
Here's the answer:
Music is áffect.' 'Affectation

Of certain never-felt sensations.'
'Ungenteel,
  Not to feel . . .'

'Try as I will,
I never can manage more than a scale.'

'Facts are facts: music's a trifle,
Something to do if you're silly and idle.'
'As for me, I greatly prefer
The tuning up, to the Overture , , ,'

'Truth is truth:
Music's uncouth,
Insult to commonsense, more shocking
Than the sight of a fishnet stocking.'

BURGOMASTER:
'All that's been said so far is – fizz!
I'll tell you what music is.

You say it's superfluous
Decoration?
Mere mellifluous
Modulations?

Music: explosions!
Music's the plague!
Burst veins, or Scythians
On the rampage!

Grab with bare hands at a burning briar!
Out of the frying pan into the fire!

Much worse than a noise in your brain,
Nightmares or fearful stories –
Music's the crash of the Stock-Exchange,
The unleashing of the Furies.

Would you invite Pope Pius to tea
At your nice suburban Christmas?
Quartet of the elements!
Wild beasts set free!

Bedrock of all slavishness:
Music is mutiny: nothing less.

Revolt of archangels, of cattle,
Of the hallway's silver stitches,
Of brides who sit at pianos (tattered
Veils!): not brides – witches!

Be kind to cardsharpers if you dare,
Not to musicians! A snooze
In a chair? It's demons on Parliament Square,
And roaming all over your house.

Diminished fifth of femaleness –
Music's the Devil: nothing less.

Goggle-eyed schoolboys with unkempt hair
Shaking their fists at Potsdam.
What is music? It's "*ça ira*"!
That's the scale of its programme!

Feathered as birds of Paradise, Hell's
Demons: "*stirb und tödte!*"
Music? The terror privately felt
By Privy Councillor Goethe

Before Beethoven.'

Eyebrows go up,
Noses go red,
Council goes 'cough!',
Scratches its head.

They sneeze,
They gulp,
They wheeze.
'God help!'

Only one, a certain talent
Not accorded recognition,
Represents Romanticism.

Rosy as a babe, this fellow,
Rejoicing in the nickname Philo-
mela, says in phrases gallant:

'A moderate dose of music's charm
Will not do us any harm.'

Grand the Burgo- , cold the -master:
'There, of course, we have the artist.'

ROMANTIC COUNCILLOR:
'*Tempi passati . . .*'

BURGOMASTER:
'Gentlemen, please be
Seated. No flippancy.

Now, do we really
(Parliament, parlez!)

Give a musician – mysterious indeed be

The ways of the Lord –
Our own flesh and blood?'

————————

The town of . . . but Hamlin is one big family!
So then: the family of Hamlin
Doesn't use 'I' as a pronoun, ever,
Unless it's all 'I's together.

Except in the case of a tangible good,
'I' equals EVERIMAN: a word

Deserving of praise, and it does infer
Value – it fits like a fur!

Yet to this writer of humble lines –
Shower me with gold till I die! –
Only one letter within it – mine! –
Has any meaning: the 'I'.

In-vincible! Thus a diamond
Lives through the blackness of fire.
Un-repeatable! What is 'I', then?
Something that can't be a pair.

In lost races' tongues
'Az' means: 'once'.

(As the
Azras . . .)

Only A, B and C live in Hamlin . . .
Here we must hold our tongue.
Word more dreadful than dinner guests guzzling
And tempests all night long:

I! (In the over-gorging majority
I means – everybody.)

Keep up with the Joneses. Follow your neighbours.
'Not for me to decide.'
The author, however, clairvoyant of lies,
With eyes as sharp as sabres,

Perceives in 'everyone' only the 'one'.
I trust you appreciate my pun.

I is an apple tree laden with fruit
To the brim: you can't pick the whole tree!
But Hamlin, instead of 'I', says 'we',
Which pronoun is only true –

And not deaf-and-dumb, a stump, a blank wall –
When each letter's six feet tall!

(Right of the giant!)
'Marry a piper?'
'How piquant!'
'Most delightful!'

Time gives way!
Space holds sway!
'Marry a clown?'
'All scruffy and brown?'

'A man with no future!'
'Tooter and fluter!'

A black goose!
Debts at the shop.
A white wolf!
House full of slop.

Parlour a puddle,
Half the roof missing.
'What is your husband?'
'He's a . . . musician.'

Rounds of applause.
Cash? Not a bit of it!
'Marry a stargazer!'
'Marry an idiot!'

Wrap your firstborn
In vision and fancy:
'Marry a hero?'
'Or is he a pansy?'

'An opus-writer!'
'A circus-rider!'

Everything pawned!
Threats of jail!
Rat-like squeal –
A chromatic scale.

Children: luggage.
Geld ist Sand.
'And your son-in-law?'
'A . . . music-man.'

Piping! Now that requires strong lungs –
All day long you'll be at it!
Not so difficult while you're young.
But when you're old and asthmatic?

Not even fit to clean out a loo!
Holding a tin? A collection,
As for the blind? The insolvent, too –
Musicians without exception!

White with wrath,
Councillors froth:
'Give the first daughter
Of the whole borough

To the first' – 'Bravo!' –
'Comer?' 'Horror!'
'To a rat-catcher?'
'To a rat-squasher?'

'Stones in his pocket?'
'Marry a convict?'

Rough coffin.
Common ditch.
No wreath,
No speech.

Dead? Then rot.
Unbekannt.
'Who was that?'
'A *Mu-sik-ant.*'

In dire embarrassment we see
The little eyes so buttery,
The lips so bow-like (usually),
Of our Romanticist. Says he:

'Blisses of Heaven do not belong
In earth-endowed Hamlin. Marriage
Of Hamlin to genius would be as wrong
As a nightingale's to a cabbage.

"To the Rose" goes the love of the nightingale.
Betraying hearth and homestead,

I shed tears over my nightingale,
But my nightingale is married!

Hamlin and genius? Where's your tact?
They're in different keys! How awful!
Is there a more unacceptable fact
Than a nightingale in lawful . . .

Wedlock means the end of your dreams:
Recumbent, with plenty of pork.
Ethereal souls never talk in that vein –
Friends, that is bürgerlich talk!

I'd gladly stand in the burgo's shoes,
But I'm – a suburban boor!
Why would a heavenly spirit choose
Him for a father-in-law?

Fame for him is significant form
Or noblehearted verse.
Why be heir to a mayor when you're born
To be lord of the universe?

A kitchen?
A doll?
A ring?
And that's all?

Hymen's not meant for the lyrical poet –
Even a child knows this.
Sobered-up nightingales, slow and sedate,
Aren't supposed to exist.

When you ethereals live here below,
Not even a patch for a hole
Is your own, for all earthly goods long ago
Were distributed rightly and well.

We received only the visible world,
You – all the rest ("where no sickness . . .").

Gods shouldn't trespass where butchers hold
Sway, nor we – where a goddess . . .

Your role: preside over everything. Ours:
Propagate – twins and triplets.
Here a contented musician appears
Absolutely illicit.

So don't begrudge to us everyday
Folk some succulent morsel!
Your ambrosia is sweeter than maids'
Lips, your nectar's immortal.

Mystics trapped in the mud of the street,
Gods in the fug of brothels –
Weep and keep vigil so we may sleep,
Die, so we can be fruitful!

As for the Burgomaster's girl,
That's a terrestrial idea!
We'll think up another. But I'm a churl
In such matters – I'll wait to hear

My colleagues' opinions . . .'

The councillors reddened and frowned with the strain,
Bulging with brows and ears.
No one in Hamlin has thoughts of his own,
Only others can have ideas.

This isn't strange: they're not up in the clouds
But on earth, when all's said and done.
And others' ideas aren't around in crowds –
In fact there is only one:

The author's . . . A whisper begins to spread:
'What shall we give him instead?'

'Something he'll use!'
'Fishing-rod!' 'Shoes

(Cheap ones)!' 'Assorted
Watch-holders.' 'Portrait

To hang on the wall!'
'Oils! For example

The kaiser on horseback!'
'Price is no obstacle!'

'A safety-razor!'
'A music-folder!'
'A walking-stick!'
'A cape for his shoulders!'

'Something small, anyway!'
'To use every day!'
'Well, we're not at Court!'
'What counts is the thought!'

'Needn't be much at all!'
'Could be quite minimal!'
'If he'd a jacket an
Iron would be feasible:

So inexpensive and
Durable!' 'Best thing is
Try to impress him. For
Him it's the gesture that . . .'

'Why be extravagant?'
'Cheap is best! 'Mustn't waste
Funds: a certificate
Stating his competence!'

'Money is tasteless.
From capers and oysters
You only get illnesses.'
'Dreams nourish geniuses.'

'Our good opinion
Is what his heart's set on:
A purse of praises.' 'Mere
Mortals would ask for more.'

'So then – a nice testimonial it is.'

ROMANTIC COUNCILLOR:
'Got it! Eureka! Applauses!
Since the vocation of flute-playing is his,
Give him a flute-case! It's obvious!'

All – clap!
Councillors – ap-
plaud: 'Brains!'
'Highbrow chap!'

Geben – frisst.
Leb' heisst spar' . . .
Won't resist –
He's a star.

'Solved!' 'Agreed!'
'Leather!' 'Suede!'

'To someone who's musical
Plush too's agreeable.'

'Plush, then!' 'Now, Council, our
Dinner will spoil!'
'Flannel's soft too – if soft
Cloth is the goal.'

'Intention's what matters most.'
'Not too much extra cost.
Let it be from the heart –
Papier-mâché, of course!'

Were there the tiniest use in a soul
Who'd be without one? Good,
So translate papier-mâché and you'll
Find that it's paper chewed.

I'm not a cow but I'll give it a chew!
Gods – but we can shut
Their mouths with (do as critics do
To nightingales) paper cud.

'Pure! No additives!'
'Passed! We're all positive!'

'Any old kind!'
'Bravo! It's signed!'

BURGOMASTER:
'So! Not my son–in–law!
Yet we may honour the
Piper as man:
Councillors, stand!

Here is the Council's decree
(A sensible spender is she):

Hamlin's no realm of the soul.
A piper's no husband at all.
Nor son–in–law. So she,
The lady mentioned, must be
Withheld. (In the realm of price!)
But we bestow, in her place,
From the realm of all that's divine,
A case for your instrument, made

Of mashed–up paper. As said
Goethe, "All things are but signs",
And what really counts, anyhow,
Is not the what but the how.'

Fur-quiet.
Lion-quiet.
Lips smile.
Drows wild.

Above stars,
Above words,
At full stature –
The Ratcatcher.

'A minstrel is always a wastrel.
A fifer won't guard his fife.
Let it crack – he'll whistle.
He is the hater of packings.
He is the smasher of wrappings.
Naked the music-maker,

Sheer. Does beauty require
Shielding? It's cankers we hide.
He is the ripper of wrappers
Off everything under the sky!

Ugly? Trample it down.
So that the essence can shine.

In your hearing, not in your ears,
Will the trumpet call you to prayers
On that day when the spirit casts
Off its flesh, the last mask,

That day when the ice stops flowing.
In your soul – with *no* trumpet blowing.

Break all the flutes! It's in us,
Not in them, that sounds are sung.
Most seeing of all is the one
Who sees without eyes. The most

Grateful and resonant hall
Is our breast. Never too small.

Nightingales don't dose
('Three drops at night!') their throats.
So stuff that case in the stove
Or dangle it on your nose . . .

Council! My prize, your debt,
Is the Burgo's daughter. I wait.'

They started to whisper: 'ps – ps – ps . . .
What, just for catching a dozen – rats?

Just for a dozen wretched – mice!
Of course he'll no sooner have this prize

Than see his own ears.'
               O Greta, a snare!
Easier to catch a glimpse of your ear

Than behold your soul.
              'Rushes, rustle!
No sooner than see your own soul.'

CANTO 6 The Children's Paradise

Roses are red, brawn is bare,
And the alarm-clock's *un-fair*.

School! School! School! School!
North-East blowing down your cagoul.

Minute your eyelid opens –
Lessons, lessons, lessons.

Warm as toast, all snug and warm –
'Ding – ding!' goes the alarm!

Force them open, tight-shut eyes –
Rise, rise, rise, rise!

Get a hold on your brains and heart!
Dark, dark, dark, dark!

Feet – in the tub.
Hands on the tap.

Make-believe's over, doldrums begin.
Lather the bloom of sleep from your skin.

The Hun, the Goth . . .
Yet to tell the truth –

What's left of the Goth-and-the-Hun's small
World? A mark in your book – that's all.

A mark, a hum . . .
A Gaul, a Hun . . .

(I'll be told off!)
A Gaul, a Goth.

Goth and Gaul.
'Too small –'
Goth and Hun.
' – my buttered bun.'

Huns are horsemen, their legs are bowed.
Four and twenty feet in a pound.
A plus and a minus make a plus.
Caesar's a German . . . I'll soon wake up.

Logs sleep, so does a bear.
Go to sleep again if you dare!

Hindus sleep, so do the dead.
I'll sleep too, I'll stay in bed.

Eyes – slits:
Alphabet bits
Like a hundred wasps'll
Get up my nostril.

For a hundred years, without a stop,
I'm wound up, wound up, wound up.

Oaks fall, thrones fall.
Wound up for good and all.

For a hundred years, without a stop . . .
And after that – what?
The one to say is the one who'll say
How to wake this clock.

What are years? What are hours?
Even volcanoes stop.
The one who knows is the one who knows
How to smash this clock.

Hours and days burn to the ground.
Still the alarm-clock's safe and sound.

Hills replace
Vale and hollow.
School today,
Office tomorrow.

Where's that busy
Bee, the swot?
School today,
Tomorrow we rot.

More tiresome than a mosquito's noise . . .
'School – boys!'

What's that? A new sound!
Books – fly – out of hand
Fast – into the fire.
Arms – higher and higher.

Tears – eyes on the blink.
Lard – falls in the sink.
Soap – falls in the soup.
(Schoolboy's *Morgensupp*'.)

Sounds! Sounds! Pouring down
As if from eyes! As if from clouds!
A flute has begun – a flute, a flute –
To pour out tunes . . .

Galloping, galloping, as from stalls,
Clattering, stamping, a rush and a roll
'Flute, play to us, flute, flow to us!' –
Of calves and heifers and kids and foals –

Runaways,
Trot-aways,
Schoolgirls and
Schoolboys.

Drops from tree-tops,
Scree from hill-tops,
Peas from garrets:
Speeding infants.

Pupil? Bosh! Report-book? Gone!
Pelting, pelting, like a drum.

Globe? Smashed! Satchel? Disowned!
Pebbles, pebbles, crashing down.

Splashing from a hundred buckets,
Atlas, wither! Crayon, wait!
Hares and jays are in the thicket,
White blackbirds in the glade.

Shouting, yelling! In such guise –
Gaping lips and gullets wide –
Savages swallow saintly lives,
Adding missionary for spice.

Child – ren!
Little gnats of the evening, all golden . . .
Wild men!
From your tuneful ponds, little gudgeon . . .

Leave your holes!
A butterfly's not a beaver . . .
Leave your schools!
A primrose won't bloom for ever . . .

Look what I've got for you – all you've been wishing:
Dolls for the girls and guns for the boys –
Excellent places for rowing and fishing –
Thimbles for girls, and skittles for boys.

Frocks, helmets . . .
Waffles, biscuits . . .

A grove for the songbirds, a lake for the fishes –
Whatever your ages, whatever your wishes.

For little ones – smarties, for bigger ones – chocolates,
Whatever you long for, whatever your secrets.

Sharp on the eyes – a sheen:
Sesame and Eden.

In your parents' home,
Did you hear the insomniac tom-tom?

Under their roof,
Who tasted the sherbet of truth?

Houses: cramped hives
For lions and for wives.

I promised, and here's my hand on it – ready:
Steeds for the boys, for the girls – does,
Fruits of Solomon, Saadi's rose,
Wars for the boys, and for girls – weddings,

The whole world ringing with song –
Caresses for everyone.

Little fish in your puddle! Birds in your cage!
Let's put an end to assessments and grades!

For birds a whole summer, a lake for the fish –
And all school subjects – smashed to bits!

In a school extremely ancient –
Heaps and heaps of Christmas presents.

'They say he's in green.' 'But where's he gone?'
'I'm following the ringing.'

'He cured my fever.' 'But where's he gone?'
'I'm following the singing.'

'I'm following a bride's red veil.'
'I'm on my elder sister's trail.'

'They say it's miles to Paradise.'
'Forgot to do my lesson – twice.'

'I'm rather scared, but I shan't confess.'
'I want to go to a faraway place.'

'I know there's something more to find.'
'I'll not stay here, not lag behind.'

'There's desperate treasure, so I've heard.'
'I'm off to seek glory!' 'I'll stay with the herd.'

'And anyway we can't go home!'
'I'm going – to get married.' 'Me? – to roam.'

'They cane us and it isn't fair.'
'Well, all the rest are going there.'

'To sleep in a haystack just for once!'
'To be with the crowd.' 'To be with Franz.'

'I want to fight the lions, see.'
'Don't know, my feet are taking me.'

'Because my Daddy pulls my hair.'
'Because everything is going there.'

Even a slapping is followed by sweets –
Rattles for all the infants –
Stories to keep the pastor in fits,
Romances for adolescents –

Everyone's fancies, everyone's needs!
Boys get bullets and girls get beads.
Everyone's longings, everyone's aims!
For girls – passions, for boys – games.

No squabble or squall,
Billets-doux for you all . . .

'I've heard it said
We'll be led round and round . . .'
(Little folk, turn round, go home!)

'And we'll end up dead,
We'll end up drowned . . .'
'Since it *can't* be worse, it won't!'

'He can't be a baddie, he plays so well!'
'And who cares if he takes us to hell –

At least there won't be sermons there!'
'Good thing we're all in a crowd.' 'I declare . . .

(There's music's coming, but where is *he*?
(And is it from sky or sea?)

. . . I can't hear any tooting or trilling:
I'm going with everyone, just to show willing.'

I've all you desire – except for a salary –
Boys will have flints, girls will have jewellery –
Magical numbers and badges and toys,
Sounds for the girls and meanings for boys.

Everything chimes,
Everything rhymes.

The wind in your coats
As you pass the school gates!

Like a circus march,
As you pass by the church!

You who never were loving,
Always bossing, shoving –
Goodbye, master!
Goodbye, pastor!

'We're not going to write, and don't you write!'
Come on, little mites!

I'll give you anything – words can't begin . . .
Pleasure for boys, and for girls – heavy care . . .
(Outlove him, outwit him – somehow you'll win)
Joys for the boys, for the girls – despair.

An end to earthly passion.
And just for one girl – heaven.

Here – fetters,
Numbers and letters,
Ruination,
Separation.

Heaven of being,
Heaven of meaning,
Heaven of sounding,
Heaven of hearing.

Like a feathery cloud – a mutter:
'That's the Burgomaster's Greta!'

Look lively, bridesmaids, line up ready
In procession for the wedding!

Time to forget the greasy markbook –
Take the younger ones by the hand.

School is just a grain of buckwheat!
Babies newly from the storkbeak –

Carry them, don't relent . . .
'Don't repent!'

A chiming sound . . .
'Don't look round!'

See – becoming space and birdflock –
Here's the edge of town.

Over-grow,
Footprints. 'We're off to Peking.'
Over-caw,
Crows, all we say or we sing.

Bushes, you,
Keep not a shred of our caps.
Breezes, you,
Scatter our voices and steps.

Leave no trace!
Wednesday – a workday for them.
In our new place
It's Sunday forever, amen.

Life means: grow
Old and decrepit and hoar.
Life's for our foe!
Timelessness waits – on that shore!

In my realm there's no murder or prison.
Blue light, icy prisms!
And under the ripples, the roof of rain –
Pearls for the girls, and for boys the game

Of diving after them: each like a ball!
And – a bath for you all.

Sleep, slip under
To pearls of wonder.

Sticks are grey – d'you want them red?
No more brushwood – coral instead.

In my kingdom, no mumps and no measles,
No lofty matters, no tales medieval,
No racial discord, no Hus at the stake,
No childhood illness or childish quake.

Blueness. The summer is fine.
All things have plenty of time.

Hush now, children, for you are going
To school underwater, all softly flowing.

Sink down, little rosy faces,
To eternal watery places.

'The slime!' 'A net!'
'My toes are wet!'

'A roar!' 'A wave!'
'The taste of lake!'

Now the water swells and steals
Over the little swimmers' heels.

Wets the ankles – pearly bright,
Laps those little divers' feet . . .

Rising over slender thighs –
'Chrys-o-lite!'

Orange mosses, azure niches . . .
(Feet sink lower, sky climbs higher)
Halls of crystal, mirrored couches . . .
Further, further, nearer, nearer . . .

'Look out! It's up to your waist!'
'Chrys-o-prase!'

Now the water laps the shoulders
Of these mice in chequered schoolclothes.

Noses afloat!
Up to the throat.

Rising and rising –
Nicer than lying

Tucked up in a cot –
'Crys-tal . . .'

In my kingdom (no voice ever sweeter)
Time grows short, horizons – wider . . .
Baby's bonnet? Or marshland seagull?
Feet grow heavy, heart grows lighter . . .

Don't forget us, friends and kin!
Water up to every chin.

Has the beggar built a castle
Fitting for the burgo-damsel?

Endless dreams and trackless hollows . . .
The heart ever quieter, the flute ever sweeter . . .
Don't think, just listen, don't think, just follow . . .
Flute ever sweeter, heart ever sleepier . . .

'Mother, you needn't call us to supper!'

Bub – bles.

Notes

Further Reading

Notes

Canto 1 Hamlin Town

Page 35: *Hamlin Town*
For convenience I am adopting, but in modified form, Browning's English version of the German name: his 'Hamelin' might suggest that the 'a' is to be pronounced as in 'same', or that the word has three syllables, so I have dropped the 'e', which is in any case redundant as our 'i' stands in for the 'e' of 'Hameln'.

The German place-name 'Hameln' is, in Russian orthography, which has no H, 'Gameln'. Tsvetaeva spells it, however, with two 'm's; it thus becomes associated with 'Hammel(fleisch)', the German for 'mutton', an association she does explicitly make in Canto 4 with a reference to 'Hammelbraten' (see note below). (According to German etymologists, 'Hameln' actually derives either from the name of a river or from the Old High German *hamma*, a corner formed by river and coast.) Imagery of 'rottenness' occurs several times in the course of the *poema* and it is likely that with the spelling 'Gammeln' Tsvetaeva also had in mind the verb 'vergammeln': to rot.

Page 36: *George*
Several commentators say this means the Russian national saint, St George the Victory-Bringer (Georgy pobedonosets), a saint Tsvetaeva admired. It must also, though, be an allusion to her just-born son (see note below).

Page 36: *proud sound*
An allusion to the well-known phrase 'Man: that sounds proud' in Maxim Gorky's play *Na dne* (The Lower Depths).

Page 37: *'Set eyes on Hamlin . . .'*
Paraphrase of 'See Naples and die'.

Page 37: *Juri . . . Rührei . . . rühr uns nicht / An*
'Juri . . . scrambled eggs . . . touch us not.' The word 'Juri' could be taken as an emblem of Tsvetaeva's macaronism. Though she has put it in a list of German words, it is neither 'Jury' meaning 'jury', nor 'Jura' meaning 'study of law', nor indeed any German word at all. It is the German spelling of what in English spelling would be 'Yury' or 'Yuriy', the affectionate form of the name Georgy

(George). This is the name Tsvetaeva had just given her neonate son (mentioned at two other places in *The Ratcatcher*), whom she would probably have addressed as Juri (Yury) and Jurochka (Yurochka) had she not decided to call him 'Mur' – whereby she probably had in mind E.T.A. Hoffmann's 'Kater Murr' (Murr the Cat), a favourite German tale of hers, and was not at all thinking of the coincidence of this name, spelt, as it is, with a single 'r', with the Latin for 'mouse' or 'rat': *mus: muris* (preserved in the English adjective 'murine').

Page 38: *Bulbas*
Taras Bulba, a Ukrainian hero and the main character in Gogol's story of that name, wears his hair in Ukrainian-Cossack style, with a tuft hanging over the forehead: symbol of masculine honour.

Page 38: *Mensch, wo bist du? . . . Bin nackt.*
'Man, where are you? . . . I am naked.' Cf. Genesis 3. 9-10: 'And the Lord God called unto Adam, and said unto him, Where art thou? And he said, I heard thy voice in the garden, and I was afraid, because I was naked; and I hid myself.'

Page 38: *Bedlams*
Bedlam – name of a well-known mental hospital in London.

Page 38: *Sansculottes*
Name applied to extreme Republicans in the French Revolution who, being poor, wore trousers, not kneebreeches (culottes).

Page 38: *Pugachov*
Yemelyan Pugachov (c. 1744-75), leader of a widespread peasant revolt against the throne; much admired by Tsvetaeva, who writes of him also in her essays 'Pushkin and Pugachov' and 'Art in the Light of Conscience'.

Page 38: *Saint-Just*
Louis-Antoine Saint-Just (1767-94), one of the ideological leaders of the French Revolution who briefly held power with Robespierre and was executed.

Page 39: *my Russky*
Here Tsvetaeva herself supplied the following footnote: 'My son Georgy (Mur), born at the height of the dream about the Ratcatcher and of its first chapter – on February 1st 1925, Sunday, exactly at noon, in a mad (the last) snowstorm, in a hut in the village of Všenory near Prague.'

Page 40: *neither / Cold nor hot*
Cf. Revelation 3.16: 'So then because thou art lukewarm, and neither cold nor hot, I will spue thee out of my mouth.'

Page 41: *'Morgen ist auch ein Tag'*
'Tomorrow is another day.'

CANTO 2   The Dreams

Page 43: *Kaspar*
German name, which to Tsvetaeva suggests a good law-abiding citizen.

Page 43: *lord of the castle . . . his servants*
Literally: 'the Burgomaster . . . his serfs'. The Russian for 'serf' is *krepostnoy*, and 'castle (fortress)' is *krepost'*; Tsvetaeva supplies a footnote here saying: ' "Burg" is German for *krepost'*.'

Page 46: *red cockerel*
conflagration (a frequent symbol in Russian folklore).

Page 46: *In other cities*
Moscow, with the red walls of its Kremlin, is implied.

CANTO 3   The Affliction

Page 51: *Zuviel ist ungesund*
'Excess is unhealthy.'

Page 52: *Tugendbund*
'League of Virtue': a patriotic (i.e. anti-Napoleonic) society in Germany in the early nineteenth century.

Page 53: *To you, the greasy and mean*
At the word preceding this Tsvetaeva puts an asterisk and a footnote explaining: 'In the following lines the first, second and last syllables are to be stressed.' In the Russian the following twelve lines can be read accordingly, i.e. with the rhythm $--\smallsmile\smallsmile-$. This does not work in English, though I have tried to approximate this rhythm. Two of my lines, 'Rats' pattering feet' and 'Rats trot down the street', do match it.

Page 54: *Zands*
Karl Ludwig Sand (which I here spell 'Zand', the way it is spelt in Russian, so as to distinguish it as a name), 1795-1820, was a nationalist (as well as progressive) student who murdered the German playwright August von Kotzebue in 1819, believing him to be in the pay of the tsar; he was executed.

Page 55: *Schande*
'Shame'.

Page 55: *Ham*
The Russian word *kham* (again related to 'Hamlin') means a boorish person as well as being the name of a son of the biblical Noah. So the Hamliners are saying that if you accuse the rat-Bolsheviks of being boorish (*kham*) they will pretend to have heard the name of a son of Noah and will reply with that of another of his sons, suggesting that, like Noah's family, they are among the few to be saved.

Page 57: *'Brot'*
'bread'.

Page 57: *'prod-'*
i.e. *produkty*: groceries, foodstuffs.

Page 57: *'kom –' / 'intern'*
Reference to the Comintern, or Communist International Association of Working Men, established by the Russians in March 1919 (it officially ended in 1943) to work towards socialist revolution throughout Europe. Meanwhile the way Tsvetaeva divides the word up brings about *kom*, a lump or clod.

Page 57: *Devkomdung*
Characteristic of official language in Soviet times was the constructing of portmanteau words for institutions and official positions by putting together the first syllables of several words. Here I suggest 'Devil's Commissar of Dung' for Tsvetaeva's *Narkomchort* and *Narkomshish* (People's Commissar of Devils, People's Commissar of Rude Signs).

CANTO 4   The Abduction

Page 63: *bashlyk*
A hood worn by soldiers, e.g. in the Civil War.

Page 63: *Karlsbad*
A health resort visited by wealthy Russians before the Revolution. Here a sign of the continuing disagreement among the rats is that some want to go to a relaxing spa, others to the centre of revolution, Moscow.

Page 64: *vint*
A card game similar to auction bridge.

Page 66: *Lying in the ditches*
Apparently a reference to the fact that White Army soldiers fleeing from their final defeat left their weapons lying about in the countryside.

Page 66: *Perekop*
Place of the decisive battle between the Whites and the Reds, with the latter triumphant.

Page 66: *lindens / Three hundred years old*
This is often taken to mean the main street in Berlin, Unter den Linden, but according to Ye. B. Korkina (see 'Note on Text and Publication') it is more likely to refer to the three hundred years of the tsarist dynasty of the Romanovs, overthrown in 1917, and to the lime-trees along the avenues of aristocratic estates.

Page 67: *Pacific-Ocean*
A geographical error to be attributed to the rats.

Page 67: *Sturm und Drang*
'Storm and Stress': Romantic movement in German literature towards the end of the eighteenth century, to which the young Goethe and Schiller adhered.

Page 68: *Shiraz*
Town in Iran/Persia, the birthplace of the poets Hafiz and Saadi, and famous for its roses.

Page 69: *blue-blooded names*
Tsvetaeva may well have in mind the noble-born Decembrists exiled to Siberia after the failed uprising of 1825, or their descendants still living in Siberia.

Page 70: *Wrong sights*
The German and Swedish translators of *The Ratcatcher* have understood the repeated words *ne te* to mean 'different'; they seem to me to mean something between 'wrong' and 'different', and my 'wrong' here should be understood as 'wrong in relation to the normal world', 'changed', as in Wallace Stevens' lines: 'Things as they are / Are changed upon the blue guitar'. The rats have not yet accepted the world changed by the music, but are in the process of doing so, as becomes clear eighteen stanzas later when the voice of, presumably, the sceptical 'old rat' utters one line: 'I tell you: those are the wrong hills!'

Page 71: *Hammelbraten*
'Roast mutton'.

Page 72: *Scythia*
An ancient region extending over a large part of European and Asiatic Russia, which many Russians of Tsvetaeva's time, especially those of the 'Eurasian' tendency, used as a symbol of the conjunction of the European and the Asiatic in the Russian.

Page 74: *Hinny*
Offspring of a she-ass and a stallion.

Page 78: *Trug und Schand*
'Deceit and shame'.

CANTO 5 In the Town Hall

Page 80: *"I'd be a cook . . ."*
Apparently a paraphrase of the words of Alexander of Macedon: 'If I weren't Alexander I'd like to be Diogenes.'

Page 83: *Hans the Gans . . .*
The very common German name 'Hans' is necessarily written in Russian as 'Gans', which happens to be the German for 'goose'.

Page 87: *Diminished fifth*
The augmented fourth or diminished fifth (a musical interval) was proscribed by medieval music theorists as 'diabolus in musica'.

Page 87: *Potsdam*
Residence of the Prussian kings.

Page 87: *"ça ira"*
This refers to the song which became a rallying-cry under the Terror (in the French Revolution) and which contains the refrain: 'Ah ça ira, ça ira, les aristocrates à la lanterne, Ah ça ira, ça ira, les aristocrates on les pendera.'

Page 87: *"stirb und tödte"*
'die and kill'. A cynical variant of the phrase 'stirb und werde' (die and become) in Goethe's poem 'Selige Sehnsucht'.

Page 87: *Goethe . . . Beethoven*
This may allude to an occasion in about 1810 when Goethe and Beethoven (who were acquainted) had to pass a group of members of the Imperial Court, whereupon Goethe removed his hat and stood aside with bowed head, but

Beethoven walked with folded arms straight through the imperial group, making some of them step aside.

Page 87: *Philomela*
Poetic name for the nightingale, from the myth about the transformation of the maiden Philomela into a nightingale.

Page 88: *Tempi passati*
'Times past'.

Page 89: *'Az'*
The Slavonic word for the first person pronoun, 'I' (in modern Russian – 'ya'); also the first letter of the Slavonic alphabet.

Page 89: *Azras*
A mythical tribe in which the young men died when they fell in love. Heine wrote a poem about this, 'Der Asra', known to Tsvetaeva.

Page 89: *Perceives in 'everyone' only the 'one'*
A literal translation would be 'Perceives in the word "everyone" only one letter, the "yat".'
    The 'e' in the Russian word for 'everyone' (*vse*) used to be written with a different letter, known as 'yat' – this was one of the letters removed from the alphabet shortly after the Revolution to simplify Russian spelling. Tsvetaeva always clung to the old orthography and takes the opportunity here to say so. Rather than produce a wholly opaque stanza I have made it refer to the syllable 'one' in 'everyone'.

Page 89: *six feet tall*
On the assumption that Tsvetaeva is thinking here of Mayakovsky, with his physical height, his often shouted verse and his adoption of the Soviet cause, for which he wrote and drew slogans, I have changed 'arshin' (about 71 centimetres) to 'six feet'. So while she may mean the size of the letters, I have added the idea of the poet's own height.

Page 90: *Geld ist Sand*
'Money is sand'.

Page 91: *Unbekannt*
'Unknown'.

Page 91: *Musikant*
'musician'.

Page 92: *bürgerlich*
'bourgeois'.

Page 92: *Hymen*
The god of marriage.

Page 92: *"where no sickness . . ."*
Words from the Orthodox funeral service.

Page 95: *Geben – frisst, / Leb' heisst spar'*
'Giving eats [away your goods], [To] live means [to] save [up].'

Page 96: *"All things are but signs"*
A deliberate misquotation of the words from the end of Goethe's *Faust*, Part II: 'Alles Vergängliche / Ist nur ein Gleichnis' ('Everything transitory is only a likeness'), words often dwelt on by Symbolist poets.

Page 97: *when the ice stops flowing*
i.e. when everything freezes over.

CANTO 6 The Children's Paradise

Page 101: *Morgensupp'*
Breakfast broth.

Page 103: *Saadi*
The thirteenth-century Persian poet, especially famous for his book of poetry called 'Gulistan' ('The rose garden').

Page 107: *Hus*
Jan Hus (1369-1415), the great Czech religious reformer, burnt at the stake for heresy.

Page 108: *Chrysolite . . . Chrysoprase*
Names for various green and golden-green semi-precious stones.

Further Reading

English translations of Tsvetaeva's verse

All the following are well worth reading: (1) *Selected Poems*, translated by Elaine Feinstein, London 1971, 6th edition 1999 (c. 90 poems). (2) *The Demesne of the Swans*, translated by Robin Kemball, Ann Arbor 1980 (62 poems) – these are the poems about the White Army mentioned in my Introduction; the volume contains an interesting essay on Russian versification and four pages of analysis of metres and stanza forms. (3) *Selected Poems*, translated by David McDuff, Newcastle-upon-Tyne 1987 (88 poems). (4) *In the Inmost Hour of the Soul. Selected Poems* translated by Nina Kossman, New Jersey 1989 (108 poems); *Poem of the End: Selected Narrative and Lyrical Poems* by the same translator, including 'Poem of the End', 'New Year's Greeting' (addressed to Rilke) and 'Poem of the Air', Dana Point CA 1998. (5) *After Russia*, translated by Michael Naydan with Slava Yastremski, Ann Arbor 1992 (152 poems). These translators represent a variety of approaches, and to sample them all might be a good way to build up a sense of the originals' quality.

Translations of Tsvetaeva's prose

I strongly recommend reading some of the prose. Marina Tsvetaeva, *A Captive Spirit: Selected Prose*, translated by Janet Marin King, Ann Arbor 1980, reprinted London 1983 and Ann Arbor 1994, contains nineteen autobiographical pieces and one of literary criticism (namely 'Two Forest Kings', mentioned in my Introduction); the piece most closely related in theme to *The Ratcatcher* is 'Mother and Music' (pp.172-87 in the 1994 edition). In my own translation, *Art in the Light of Conscience. Eight Essays on Poetry*, Bristol 1992, also Cambridge MA 1994, I would especially recommend, as bearing on ideas implicit in *The Ratcatcher*, the following essays: 'The Poet on the Critic', 'The Poet and Time', 'Two Forest Kings' and the title piece 'Art in the Light of Conscience'. Finally, everyone interested in Tsvetaeva should surely read Boris Pasternak, Marina Tsvetayeva, Rainer Maria Rilke, *Letters 1926*, edited by Yevgeny Pasternak, Yelena Pasternak and Konstantin Azadovsky, and translated by Walter Arndt and Margaret Wettlin, London 1986 – both for the twenty letters it contains by Tsvetaeva herself and for the all-important letters Pasternak wrote to her in June and July of that year conveying his impression of *The Ratcatcher* (pp.134, 147–53 and 160–5).

Works about Tsvetaeva

Simon Karlinsky's pioneering work *Marina Cvetaeva: Her Life and Art*, Berkeley CA 1966, is still worth reading, especially for the section on versification, although it is in many ways superseded by his second book about her: *Marina Tsvetaeva: The Woman, her World and her Poetry*, Cambridge 1985 – a good introduction, both biographically and critically. Among other biographies I suggest reading (1) Viktoria Schweitzer, *Tsvetaeva*, translated by Robert Chandler and H.T. Willetts, edited by A. Livingstone and containing numerous quotations from her poetry translated by Peter Norman; and (2) Lily Feiler, *Marina Tsvetaeva, The Double Beat of Heaven and Hell*, Durham and London 1994 – a shorter, more psychologically oriented book. The study by Michael Makin, *Marina Tsvetaeva: Poetics of Appropriation*, Oxford 1993, considers her work in the light of its use of literary forerunners and traditions. G.S. Smith has written widely on Tsvetaeva's versification: I will single out 'Logoaedic Metres in the Lyric Poetry of Marina Tsvetayeva', *Slavonic and East European Review* 132, July 1975 (pp.330–54). Olga Peters Hasty has published a valuable account of Tsvetaeva's poetics, with special attention to her use of the myth of Orpheus, in *Tsvetaeva's Orphic Journeys in the Worlds of the Word*, Evanston IL 1996. Joseph Brodsky's brilliant studies of Tsvetaeva as a prose-writer and of her 'New year's *poema* to Rilke, 'A Poet and Prose' and 'Footnote to a Poem', are included in his volume of essays *Less Than One*, Harmondsworth 1986 (pp.176–94 and 195–268); Barbara Heldt, *Terrible Perfection: Women and Russian Literature*, Bloomington IN 1987 discusses Tsvetaeva as specifically a woman writer; and Sibelan Forrester, 'Marina Tsvetaeva as Literary Critic and Critic of Literary Critics', in *Russian Writers on Russian Writers*, edited by Faith Wigzell, Oxford 1994 (pp.81–98) discusses some of the essays in *Art in the Light of Conscience* cited above. Last, but certainly not least, there are two splendid studies of *The Ratcatcher* itself by Catherine Ciepiela: the one that I have skimpily summarised in my Introduction is 'Leading the Revolution: Tsvetaeva's *The Pied Piper* and Blok's *The Twelve*', in *Marina Tsvetaeva: One Hundred Years*, edited by V. Schweitzer, J. Taubman, P. Scotto and T. Babonyshev, Berkeley CA 1994. The other, 'Taking Monologism Seriously: Bakhtin and Tsvetaeva's *The Pied Piper*', *Slavic Review* LIII/4 1994 (pp.1010–24), shows how this *poema* contains both the social polyphony that for Bakhtin characterises the novel and what he less positively calls the monologism of the lyricist – which in this case triumphs over the polyphony.

Works in Russian

Students of Russian should turn to the original *poema*, for instance in the edition of Tsvetaeva's works edited by Ye.B. Korkina, Moscow 1990. Do *not* bother with the Soviet text of 1965, which was greatly shortened by the censor, nor with the British reprint of that (Letchworth, Herts 1978). Another good edition, with useful notes, is that in vol.3 of *Stikhotvoreniya i poemy v pyati tomakh* [Poems and *poemy* in five volumes], edited by A. Sumerkin, New York 1980–90. The original Russian of the prose pieces translated by J.M. King and A. Livingstone in the volumes cited above can be found in Marina Tsvetaeva, *Izbrannaya proza 1917-1937 v dvukh tomakh* [Selected prose 1917–1937 in two volumes], edited by A. Sumerkin, New York 1979; this has as its preface the original text of Brodsky's essay 'Poet i proza' [A poet and prose]. There are two books devoted to *Krysolov* – those by I. Malinkovich and T. Suni, cited in notes 15 and 30 to the Introduction. For a shorter, more concentrated study of *Krysolov*, see Ye. Etkind, cited in note 18 to the Introduction. A useful biographical work in Russian is Veronika Losskaya, *Marina Tsvetaeva v zhizni* [Marina Tsvetaeva in life], Tenafly NY 1989, which puts together substantial quotations from memoirs and letters by people who knew her, and is not difficult reading. Also recommended are Irma Kudrova, *Posle Rossii* [After Russia], Moscow 1997, a work in two volumes of which the first, *Marina Tsvetaeva. Gody chuzhbiny* [Marina Tsvetaeva. The years abroad], is about the poet's life, and the second, *Stat'i o poezii i proze Mariny Tsvetaevoy* [Articles on the poetry and prose of Marina Tsvetaeva], is about her work; and a study of her verse by L.V. Zubova, *Poeziya Mariny Tsvetaevoy; Lingvisticheskiy aspekt*, Leningrad 1989.

Also in Angel Classics (paperback)

PIERRE CORNEILLE
Horace
Translated by Alan Brownjohn
0 946162 57 3

This powerful drama, which helped launch French classical tragedy, lays bare the sinister nature of patriotism.

'Corneille's rhyming alexandrines have been superbly translated into a flexible blank verse which captures the nuances of meaning . . .' – Maya Slater, *Times Literary Supplement*

HEINRICH HEINE
Deutschland
Translated by T.J. Reed; bilingual edition
0 946162 58 1

The wittiest work of Europe's wittiest poet.

'a fine example of superior political poetry. This translation triumphantly conveys the satirical power, ironic tone and humorous accessibility.' – Anita Bunyan, *Jewish Chronicle*

'Reed's version is brilliantly successful, at times achieving what one might have thought impossible: English verse as witty and precise as the original.' – *Forum for Modern Language Studies*

JOHANN WOLFGANG VON GOETHE
Torquato Tasso
A version by Alan Brownjohn with Sandy Brownjohn; introduction by T. J. Reed
0 946162 19 0

A verse play about the moral and social problems of being a patron and being patronised. In the confrontation between poet and statesman at the cultivated court of Ferrara, Goethe's own experience is fashioned into universal conflicts.

'The claustrophobic atmosphere Goethe creates by confining his Romantic character to a Classical play makes the work structurally a metaphor of its own theme. The translation catches the breathless spirit of Tasso's soliloquies within a loose blank verse format and manages to contrast this language with the more regular and epigrammatic iambic pentameter of the courtly characters he chafes against.' – S. Plaice, *Times Literary Supplement*

For a complete list please write to Angel Books, 3 Kelross Road, London N5 2QS